T0328492

Dhaxalreeb Series 1 / 2018

Papers from the Linguistics Workshop: Somali Language and Literature at the Hargeysa Cultural Centre, December 2015

Edited by
Martin Orwin

2018

Hargeysa

PONTE INVISIBILE
WWW.REDSEA-ONLINE.COM

REDSEA Cultural Foundation
Daarta Oriental Hotel - Hargeysa, Somaliland
Telefoon: 00 252 2 525109 | 00 252 2 4099088
email: bookshop@redsea-online.com

Ponte Invisibile. Inquiries to the editor: Jama Musse Jama
Via Pietro Giordani 4, 56123, Pisa, Italy
ponteinvisibile.com | email: editor@redsea-online.com
Published by Ponte Invisibile (redsea-online), 2018, Hargeysa

Copyright ©Ponte Invisibile Edizioni 2018
A REDSEA-ONLINE Publishing Group Company.

Cover by Jama Musse Jama

ISBN 88-88934-59-6
EAN 9788888934594

Classification: 410 Linguistics
Hargeysa Cultural Centre Library (HCCL)
Catalogue Record: PL 5112 OM4303 2018

A CIP record of this book is available at HCCL, Hargeysa, Soma
liland. www.hargeysaculturalcenter.org/the-library/

www.redsea-online.com/books

Table of contents

Introduction

Martin Orwin

The articles in this book are the result of the First Linguistics Workshop: Somali Language and Literature at the Hargeysa Cultural Centre in December 2015.

The objective of the workshop was to facilitate the sharing of current work among scholars in the field of Somali language studies through presentation of their ongoing projects. This also allowed current work to be opened to a wider audience and for students, journalists and writers to hear about some of the issues which are of current interest in Somali language studies. There was a deliberate attempt to draw people engaged in both more strictly linguistic matters together with those whose interests are more as practitioners with language, such as local writers and journalists, and also to include those whose primary focus is literature.

This led to a diverse range of both presentations and opinions on those presentations, which is represented also in this volume. The views on any matter are those of the individual authors and readers are left to determine for themselves to what extent they agree or disagree with points made. The more strictly linguistic papers include presentations on aspects of Somali phonology, morphology and syntax. Sociolinguistics is also represented as is recent work on lexicography and the use of information technology in Somali language studies. There are two papers which consider literature from different perspectives.

The nature of the Somali noun phrase

Maxamed Xaaji Raabbi

Independent scholar, Hargeysa
somsynrabi@gmail.com

Abstract

This paper attempts to deal with the main features the Somali noun phrase (NP). After a brief introduction, the NP of a simple sentence is identified in section 2. Afterwards in section 3, the head of an NP (noun or pronoun) is discussed. In section 4 we consider the types of article suffixed to the head. Nouns as modifiers are looked into in section 5. The paper concludes with remarks in section 6.

1 Introduction

In traditional grammar a simple sentence has the two main parts: subject and predicate. In modern grammars, however, the two parts have been renamed as noun phrase (NP) and verb phrase (VP) respectively. Most languages share this division in their syntax. The modern terms of NP and VP are preferred to the traditional ones because they are more accurate in naming the nature of the subject and the predicate. Today an NP is defined as a phrase whose head is always a noun and a VP as a phrase whose head is always a verb, which the traditional terms do not imply.

In Somali, a noun phrase and a verb phrase have distinct features that are particular to its phraseology. A Somali basic sentence then always has a sentence particle (SP) in its declarative form, see Maxamed X. Raabbi (2009)).

2 Identifying a noun phrase

In order to identify the NP in a simple, declarative Somali sentence, we might use either of these two strategies: a) insert a pause between the NP and VP; b) delete the subject of the sentence, thus changing a declarative sentence to an imperative, for which we need to use a different form of the verb.

To apply the first rule, the Somali language does not exhibit a recognizable pause between the NP and VP. For instance, it is possible to insert a pause or a single juncture (|) before and after the SP in 1.

(1)   a. Nin | *baa*/*ayaa* hadlaya
           Man | SP   speak

           A man is speaking.

      b. Nin *baa*/*ayaa* | hadlaya
           Man SP | speak

           A man is speaking.

      c. Naagi   *waa* | joogtaa xafiiska
           Woman SP | stay   office.the

           A woman stays in the office.

      d. Naagi | *waa* joogtaa xafiiska
           Woman | SP stay   office.the

           A woman stays in the office.

In examples 1a-1d, it is not possible to judiciously decide, by asking a Somali, educated or not, whether the positions of the pauses (|) are where the subject and its predicate meet or separate. Therefore the second strategy above has to be used.

In applying this second strategy, the Somali language accepts the omission of the subject in imperative sentences. For instance, by changing the declarative sentences above (1a-1d) into imperative ones, the resulting sentences are only their predicates as in 2.

(2)   a. Hadal
           speak

           Speak!

      b. Hadal
           speak

           Speak!

    c. Joog xafiiska
       stay office.the
       Stay in the office.

    d. Joog xafiiska
       stay office.the
       Stay in the office.

In the imperative sentences in 2, the subjects of 1a-1d have been deleted, together with the particles baa, ayaa and waa, suggesting that these particles are part of the subject NPs and hence noun phrase markers. However, by shifting the subject NP (underlined in 3 below) to another position, the three particles cluster into two groups as shown in 3.[1]

(3) a. *Baa/ayaa hadlaya <u>nin</u>
      SP   speak   man
      SP is speaking a man

    b. Waa joogtaa xafiiska <u>naagi</u>
      SP stay   office.the woman
      A woman stays in the office.

Shifting subject NPs to final position renders sentence 3a incorrect and 3b correct; which means that ayaa / baa is a subject NP marker. In sentence 3b, however, the SP waa does not move with the subject NP. It remains in its relative position, which means that it is an essential part of the predicate or a verb phrase marker.

But the SP ayaa / baa can also mark other NPs, i.e. object NPs as shown in 4.

(4) a. *Xafiiska ayaa* <u>ninku</u>   joogaa
      object-NP   subject-NP
      The man stays in the office.

    b. *Beerta ayaa* <u>naagtu</u>   joogtaa
      object-NP   subject-NP
      The woman stays in the garden.

---

[1] Asterisks (*) indicate ungrammaticality.

Therefore, we can safely say that a Somali NP may fit into the frame ___ ayaa / baa ... (see 3a, 4a & 4b) and a VP may fit into the frame waa ___ ... (see 3b).

Consequently, a VP is a group of words which move together within a simple sentence and whose nucleus or head is always a verb and occurs after waa (waa ___). However an NP, which we are concerned with in this paper, is a group of words which move together within a simple sentence and whose nucleus or head is always a noun that may occur before the sentence particle ayaa / baa (___ ayaa / baa) or before waa (___ waa + verb / verb + noun).

Besides its position, a noun phrase has the basic feature of being marked versus unmarked. An indefinite NP is marked for subject in feminine nouns (1c & 1d: naag : naagi) and unmarked for masculine nouns (1a & 1b, nin : nin). A definite subject NP is, however, marked for a 'waa frame' (___ waa + verb / verb + noun) (4a: ninku, 4b: naagtu) and unmarked regardless of gender for an 'ayaa / baa frame' (___ ayaa / baa) (4a: xafiiska, 4b: beerta) as well as all other positions such as adverbials of time and place as in 5.

(5) a. *Maanta* ayaa roob da'ay
         today   SP   rain fell

         Today it rained. / It rained today.

     b. *Halkan*   baa wiilku yimid
         place.this SP boy.the came

         The boy came here.

Having identified the NP, we now consider the language elements that are part of it. The words that are part of the noun phrase can be dealt with in three stages: the head, affixes to the head and head modifiers. Theoretically, depending on the word classes (the parts of speech) which a language has, a noun phrase may consist of some or all of its word classes.

Of the three word classes (nouns, verbs and particles) the Somali language allows only nouns and some pronouns to be the head of an NP. The rest cluster around it, some affixed to it like the articles and others occurring separately after it, such as nouns, verbs and other particles as modifiers. The nature of modification in Somali NPs is, moreover, such that it is always post-positioned without exception.

3 The head of a noun phrase

The head of a Somali NP is either a noun or its substitute, a pronoun. By using the frames '__ ayaa / baa' and '__ waa+verb / verb+noun' we can capture the essential features of a Somali NP. In **waa**-sentences, subject NPs are always marked as in examples 1c and 3b above. But in those sentences with **ayaa** / **baa**, the NPs preceding **ayaa** / **baa** are unmarked as in examples 1a, 4a and 4b above. Subject NPs not preceding **ayaa** / **baa** however are still marked (see 4a and 4b). We begin with pronouns for some do serve as heads and some do not.

3.1 Pronouns as heads of NPs

3.1.1 Ayaa / baa as SP: NPs with modifying words

The words in italics are pronouns and all serve as heads of the NPs in the sentences in 6. The modifying words are underlined.

(6) a. *Ka*   <u>guriga</u>   <u>jooga</u> ayaa baabuur wada
        the.one house.the stay   SP   car   drive

        The one staying in the house drives a car.

   b. *Kii*   <u>maqnaa</u> baa jooga
        the.one away   SP stay

        The one who was away is [here].

   c. *Tee*   <u>gaaban</u> baa cusub
        which.one short   SP   new

        Which one that is short is new?

   d. *Tan*   <u>madow</u> <u>ee</u>   <u>jeexan</u> baa hadhay
        this.one black   and torn   SP is.left

        This one which is black and torn is left.

   e. *Isaga* <u>ka</u>   <u>hadlaya</u> <u>guriga</u>   ayaa cabanaya
        he   from speaking house.the SP   is.complaining

The person who is speaking from the house is complaining.

f. *Kooda* <u>yaalla qolka</u> ayaa fiican
theirs placed room SP good
Theirs in the room is good.

These six pronouns represent five categories of pronouns:

a) definite pronouns: ka, ta, kuwa, kii, tii, kuwii (6a & 6b);

b) interrogative pronouns: kee, tee, kuwee (6c);

c) demonstrative pronouns: kan, tan and kuwan (masculine, feminine and plural respectively) (6d);

d) personal pronouns: aniga, adiga, isaga etc. (6e);

e) possessive pronouns: kayga, kaaga, kooda etc.(6f).

In all six sentences above, the heads of noun phrases are accompanied by modifying words (clauses).

3.1.2   ayaa / baa as **SP: NPs without modifying words**

When we delete the modifying words from the examples in 6, the resulting sentences (given in 7) become either grammatical or ungrammatical.

(7)   a. *Ka   ayaa baabuur wada
the.one SP   car   drive

no translation

b. *Kii*   baa jooga
the.one SP stay

The one is here.

c. *Tee*   baa cusub
which.one SP new

Which one is new?

    d. *Tan*   baa hadhay
       this.one SP is.left
       This one is left.

    e. *Isaga* ayaa cabanaya
       he   SP   is.complaining
       He is complaining.

    f. *Kooda* ayaa fiican
       theirs SP   good
       Theirs is good.

7a stands out as an incorrect sentence which suggests that the pronouns ka, ta and kuwa do not occur in this linguistic environment.

3.1.3 Waa as SP: NPs with modifying words

Substituting ayaa / baa with waa in the sentences in 6 above transforms them into those in 8 below.

(8) a. *Ka*   guriga   joogaa waa wadaa baabuur
        the.one house.the stay   SP drive car
        The one staying in the house drives a car.

    b. *Kii*   maqnaa waa joogaa
       the.one away   SP stay
       The one who was away is [here].

    c. **Tee* gaabani waa cusub tahay
       which short   SP new   is
       Which one that is short is new?

    d. *Tan*   madow ee jeexani waa hadhay
       this.one black and torn   SP is.left
       This one which is black and torn is left.

    e. *Isaga* ka hadlayaa guriga   waa cabanayaa
       he   from speaking house.the SP is.complaining
       The person who is speaking from the house is complaining.

f. *Kooda* <u>yaall<u>aa</u></u> <u>qolka</u> waa fiican <u>yahay</u>
   theirs placed   room SP good   is

   Theirs in the room is good.

There are a number of changes in sentences 8a-8f. Sentence 8c stands out as incorrect. The other changes are long vowels which are double-underlined and tahay and yahay in 8c and 8f, confirming and reinforcing the concept of markedness that mostly distinguishes the '___ ayaa / baa + verb / noun + verb' frame from the '___ waa + verb / verb + noun' frame as mentioned earlier.

3.1.4 Waa as SP: NPs without modifying words

Similarly, deleting the modifying words from the sentences in 8 above results in the sentences in 9 below.

(9) a. **Ka*   waa wad<u>aa</u> baabuur
        the.one SP drive car

        no translation

  b. *Kii*   waa joo<u>gaa</u>
        the.one SP stay

        The one is here.

  c. **Tee* waa cusub <u>tahay</u>
        which SP new   is

        no translation

  d. *Tani*   waa hadhay
        this.one SP is.left

        This one is left.

  e. *Isa<u>gu</u>* waa cabanay<u>aa</u>
        he   SP is.complaining

        He is complaining.

  f. *Koo<u>du</u>* waa fiican <u>yahay</u>
        theirs SP good   is

        Theirs is good.

Sentences 9a and 9c are incorrect, which means that the definite pronouns ka, ta, kuwa and the interrogative pronouns tee, kee and kuwee do no fit into the '__ waa + verb / verb + noun' frame; but the rest are grammatical. Other changes are double-underlined indicating markedness.

3.2 Nouns as heads of NPs

We have briefly dealt with nouns, definite and indefinite, as heads of NPs in 2 (see examples in 1-4) above. Now, we will attempt to look at them more closely, using the unmarked frame only, namely '__ ayaa / baa ...' for two reasons: a) all NPs can occur before the ayaa / baa particles; b) the SP ayaa / baa serves as a limiter. The italicized words in the examples in 10 are heads of NPs for they fit into the '__ ayaa / baa ...' frame.

(10) a. *Qof*   baa cambe cunaya
         person SP mango is.eating

        A person is eating a mango.

    b. *Meeqa*   ayaa aad rabtaa
        how much/many SP   you want

        How much/many do you want?

    c. *Maanta* ayaa uu tegay
       today   SP   he went

        He went today. / Today he went.

    d. *Wasaarad* baa ku jirta sartan
       ministry   SP in is   building.this

        A ministry uses this building.

We said earlier that the Somali language consists of three types of word classes: nouns, verbs and particles (Maxamed X. Raabbi, 1994: pp.15-16). Now, we shall try to determine, one at a time, which of these can fit between the head and the SP, that is the 'head __ ayaa / baa' frame.

4 The types of article suffixed to the head noun

In Somali only articles are affixed to the nouns. All the categories of pronouns that serve as heads of NPs, mentioned in section 3.1, can serve also as language elements that can become part of the head noun apart from the personal pronouns. All the sentences in 11 share the same indefinite subject noun phrase **nin**.

(11) a. *Nin* baa baabuur raacay
      man SP   car   left.in

      A man left in a car.

   b. *Nin* baa jeeb   qalin ka   bixiyey
      man SP pocket pen   from took

      A man took a pen from a pocket.

   c. *Nin* baa xafiiska ka   baxay
      man SP office.the from left

      A man left the office.

   d. *Nin* baa buug la   baxay
      man SP book with left

      A man left with a book.

   e. *Nin* baa soo   baxay
      man SP deictic particle left

      A man came out.

Changing the indefinite head **nin** to a definite head of the subject NP transforms the sentences in 11 into those in 12.

(12) a. Nin*ka*   ayaa baabuur raacay
      man.the SP   car   left.in

      The man left in a car.

   b. Nin*kii* baa jeeb   qalin ka   bixiyey
      man.the SP pocket pen   from took

      The man took a pen from a pocket.

    c. Nin*kee*   baa xafiiska ka   baxay
       man.which SP office.the from left
       Which man left the office?

    d. Nin*keeda*   ayaa buug la   baxay
       man/husband.her SP   book with left
       Her husband left with a book.

    e. Nin*kan* baa soo   baxay
       man.this SP deictic particle left
       This man came out.

The suffixes in italics, attached to the subject NP **nin** are articles or defining linguistic elements. Somali attaches articles as suffixes to the nouns they define. The Somali language uses more than twenty words as articles. Table 1 sheds some light on the relationship between pronouns and articles.

Table 1: Relationship between pronouns and articles

Category	Pronouns			Articles (suffixed to nouns)		
1. Definite	masc.	fem.	pl.	masc.	fem.	
	ka	ta	kuwa	-ka	-ta	
	kii	tii	kuwii	-kii	-tii	
2. Interrogative	kee	tee	kuwee	-kee	-tee	
3. Demonstrative	kan	tan	kuwan	-kan	-tan	
	kaas	taas	kuwaas	-kaas	-taas	
4. Possessive	1st p.	2nd p.	3rd p.	1st p.	2nd p.	3rd p.
singular	kayga	kaaga	kiisa/keeda	-kayga	-kaaga	-kiisa/-keeda
plural	kayaga/keenna	kiinna	kooda	-kayaga/-keenna	-kiinna	-kooda/
5. Personal	1st p.	2nd p.	3rd p.			
singular	aniga	adiga	isaga/iyada	There are no corresponding articles for this category		
plural	annaga/innaga	idinka	iyaga			

5 Nouns as modifiers to heads of noun phrases

5.0.1 Adding another noun to the head

Adding another noun to the head results in sentences such as those in 13, cf. the sentences in 10.

(13) a. * *Qof* waayeel baa canbe cunaya
         person elder   SP mango is.eating
         An elder person is eating a mango.

      b. *Meeqa*   buug ayaa aad rabtaa
         how.many book SP   you want
         How many books do you want?

      c. *Maanta* salaaddii ayaa uu tegay
         today   prayer.the SP he went
         He went to prayers today.

      d. *Wasaarad* caafimaad baa ku jirta sartan
         ministry   health   SP in is   building.this
         A health ministry is in this building.

Example 13a is ungrammatical, and we will drop it from our examples. By correcting it though, we find the problem and can produce the grammatical sentence in 14.

(14) Qof   *waayeel ah* baa canbe cunaya
      person elder   is SP mango is.eating
      An elder person is eating a mango.

This sentence consists of two, collapsed into one: Qof baa waayeel ah and Qof baa canbe cunaya. The order may also be Qof canbe cunaya baa waayeel ah. The noun phrase that we are dealing in this paper is that of a basic/simple sentence, sentences with subordinate clauses do not concern us here.

5.0.2 Adding a second noun to the rest

Adding another noun to the rest gives us these grammatical NPs in 15.

(15)   a. *Meeqa*   `buug qoraal ayaa aad rabtaa`
how many book writing SP   you want
How many instances of bookwriting do you want?

   b. *Maanta* `salaaddii waaberiga ayaa uu tegay`
today   prayer.the dawn.the   SP   he went
He went to dawn prayers today.

   c. *Wasaarad* `caafimaad xoolo   baa ku jirta`
ministry   health   animals SP   in   is
`sartan`
building.this
A ministry of animal husbandry is in this building.

Example 15c 'Wasaarad caafimaad xoolo baa ku jirta sartan'
sounds both somewhat correct and incorrect. Adding articles to the
nouns makes it grammatically sound as in 16.

(16)   *Wasaaradda* `caafimaadka xoolaha      baa ku jirta`
ministry.the health.the   animals.the SP   in   is
`sartan`
building.this
The Ministry of Animal Husbandry is in this building.

This means that NPs consisting of three nouns: a head (`wasaarad`)
and two others (`caafimaad` and `xoolo`) can be ambiguous. Without
definite articles it is difficult to know whether the nouns in any NP
are in a modifying or compounding relationship. Similarly, Example
ple 15b 'Maanta salaaddii waaberiga ayaa uu tegay' consists of
three nouns that have a modifying relationship because the three
nouns have definite articles. Example 15a, however, becomes ungrammatical when articles are added to the nouns as in 17.

(17)   **Meeqa*   `buugga   qoraalka   ayaa aad rabtaa`
how many book.the writing.the SP   you want
How many the writing book do you want?

We can say, then, that the two nouns `buug` and `qoraal` are not
in a modifying relationship. Incidentally, `meeqa` is an interrogative

word in an NP position as a head and all the nouns that are part of its NP are always indefinite. What, then, is the relationship between the nouns **buug** and **qoraal** if it is not one of modification?

There are various relationships between nouns, but only two interest us at this point to limit the topic: modification and compounding. Sentence 16 'Wasaaradda caafimaadka xoolaha baa ku jirta sartan' is an example of a modification relationship because the definite articles are suffixed to the nouns in question, as we have already noticed.

The relationship between the two nouns **buug** and **qoraal** in 15a is not one of modification because the addition of two articles, **buugga qoraalka** as in Example 17, renders the sentence ungrammatical. Collapsing the two nouns into one word to form a compound gives us the sentence in 18.

(18)   *Meeqa*   buug-qoraal ayaa aad rabtaa
       how many book-writing SP   you want
       How many instances of book-writing do you want?

Sentence 18 is thus grammatical when the two nouns **buug** and **qoraal** are conjoined. Adding an article as in 19, moreover, renders the sentence ungrammatical also for the same reason that sentence 17 is ungrammatical.

(19)   **Meeqa*   buug-qoraalka ayaa aad rabtaa
       how many book-writing.the SP   you want
       How many instances of the book-writing do you want?

This means that nouns in an interrogative environment are always indefinite. Changing the interrogative sentences in 15a, 17, 18 and 19 to declaratives we get sentences such as those in 20.

(20)   a. *Buug qoraal ayaa miiska   saaran
          book writing SP   table.the placed
          A writing book is on the table.

       b. Buugga   qoraalka ayaa miiska   saaran
          book.the writing.the SP   table.the placed
          The writing book is on the table.

c. *Buug-qoraal ayaa miiska   saaran
   book-writing   SP   table.the placed

   Book-writing is on the table.

d. *Buug-qoraalka ayaa miiska   saaran
   book-writing.the SP   table.the placed

   The book-writing is on the table.

From the examples in 20, we learn that if two nouns are in a modifying relationship, they accept two articles: **buugga qoraalka** as in 20b 'the exercise book, the diary, the notebook etc.'. But if they are in a compounding relationship, they accept one article: **buug-qoraalka**, as in 20d 'the book-writing activity', which is a process, not an object, and hence cannot literally be put on a table like a notebook. That is why sentence 20d is ungrammatical.

By changing 20d into 21, we get the sentence below.

(21) *Buug-qoraalka*   ayaa baruhu   ka qaybgalay
     book-writing.the SP   teacher.the in took.part

     The teacher has taken part in the book-writing.

A compound, then, can serve as a head like in sentences 18 and 21 or a modifier as in 22.

(22) Barahan   ayaa ka qaybgalay kulankii
     teacher.this SP   in took.part   workshop.the
     buug-qoraalka
     book-writing.the

     This teacher has taken part in the book-writing workshop.

6   Concluding remarks

Moving a Somali subject NP from initial to final position in a simple sentence results in two types of subjects: marked and unmarked. The unmarked always fits into the frame 'head __ ayaa / baa + verb / noun + verb' or ayaa- / baa-sentences. The marked fits into the frame 'head __ waa + verb / verb + noun' or waa-sentences. The head of a noun phrase is either a noun or its substitute, a pronoun. If it is a noun, articles are suffixed, but definite, interrogative and demonstrative pronouns do not accept them. Besides articles being suffixed to it, a head of a noun phrase can either be a single noun or a compound. The addition of another noun to the head, without compounding, serves as a modifier. When two nouns are in a modifying relationship, they accept two articles. A compounding relationship allows one article after collapsing the two nouns into a single noun which can serve as a head or a modifier.

References

Maxamed X. Raabbi (1994). *Naxwaha Sifeyneed ee Afsoomaaliga: Ereyeynta.* No publisher.

Maxamed X. Raabbi (2009). *Qaangaadh ee qaabku waa* . . . . Djibouti: Institut des Langues de Djibouti.

Grammatical Gender and Number in Somali Nouns[1]

Morgan Nilsson

Department of Languages and Literatures, University of Gothenburg, Sweden

morgan.nilsson@gu.se

Abstract

In many of the existing textbooks and pedagogical grammars of Somali, issues related to the gender and number of nouns are presented in rather complex ways. In my experience, these descriptions and explanations are often perceived as difficult by learners of Somali grammar, both Somali speakers and foreign language learners.

I therefore argue in this article that it is possible to present the same facts in a simpler and yet precise manner. The formation of the plural of most Somali nouns, the indefinite as well as the definite form, can be handled by just a few straight-forward principles, but in order to do so, it is also necessary to carefully reconsider which forms are really plurals and which forms are actually singular forms of collective nouns.

Other closely related issues that are discussed in the article are gender polarity, uncountable nouns, *pluralia tantum*, mass nouns and corporate nouns, as well as the agreement of verbs and pronouns with nouns.

---

[1]I wish to express my sincere gratitude to the more than 50 students, all L1 speakers of Somali, in the Somali mother tongue teachers programme at the University of Gothenburg, for the many enlightening discussions and remarks during our grammar classes in 2014/2015 and 2015/2016. Abbreviations: coll. = collective; def. = definite; f. = feminine; indef. = indefinite; m. = masculine; pl. = plural; sg. = singular; sgtv. = singulative.

1 Introduction

Somali has two genders, masculine and feminine, and two numbers, singular and plural. It has two morphemes expressing definiteness, {k} and {t}.[2] Each morpheme is traditionally tightly associated with one gender, {k} with masculine gender and {t} with feminine gender. The actual realisation of these morphemes depends on the stem-final phoneme: {k} is realised as either /k/, /g/, /h/ or zero, whereas {t} is realised as either /t/, /d/, /ɖ/ or /ʃ/.

The same two morphemes are used both in the singular and in the plural, and the majority of Somali nouns take the opposite morpheme in the plural compared to the morpheme that they take in the singular. This is traditionally interpreted as a change of gender so that the plural form of a noun has the opposite gender when compared to the singular form of the same noun. For this phenomenon, the notion of GENDER POLARITY is applied, explicitly or implicitly, in most descriptions of Somali grammar, meaning that all nouns that are feminine and take the article {t} in the singular become masculine and take the article {k} in the plural, whereas most nouns that are masculine and take the article {k} in the singular become feminine and take the article {t} in the plural. Only a smaller group of nouns, which are masculine in the singular, remain masculine also in the plural and hence take the article {k} irrespective of their number. This means that a distinct gender value has to be associated with the plural form of nouns, and that the definite article is then assigned according to the plural gender of each specific noun (El-Solami-Mewis (1988), Saeed (1999: 54–5), Berchem (2012: 48–9) among others). Lecarme (2002), however, suggests that the gender value is instead associated with the individual plural morphemes and that it is the plural morpheme that bears the gender value in the plural forms of nouns, not the nouns themselves.

This standard point of view is illustrated in Table 1. It is applied in practically all modern reference works on Somali grammar, also by Moreno (1955), Saeed (1993), Maxamed X. Raabbi (1994),

---

[2]Curly brackets indicate underlying morphemes that are realised differently in different phonological contexts.

Puglielli and Abdalla Omar Mansur (1999), Omer Haji Bile Aden (2009), Alejnikov (2012) and others.

Table 1: Gender polarity: the traditional view of gender in Somali nouns

	SINGULAR	PLURAL	
FEMININE	{t}	{k}	MASCULINE
MASCULINE	{k}	{t}	FEMININE

The horizontal line in the middle of the table is discontinuous as some nouns are masculine in both numbers.

In Section 2, I will however argue that the form of the plural definite article is morphologically predictable without reference to plural gender. The exact principles for the distribution of the definite article suffixes in the plural will be discussed in detail in Section 4.

2 Plural gender

Two basic questions for the description of Somali gender and number are: What purposes does the gender value in nouns serve in the description of Somali? Is there an actual need for a specific gender value in plural nouns?

Of course, for nouns in the singular, the gender value of a noun is indispensable in order to choose the correct agreement form of pronouns and verbs, as well as to choose the correct form of the definite article suffix to be added to the noun itself. In the plural, however, the gender value is not needed in order to choose a specific agreement form for pronouns or verbs, as no gender distinction exists in the plural forms of pronouns and verbs, as shown in Table 2. There exist other tenses and moods of verbs and other types of pronouns, besides those listed in the table. The pattern, however, remains the same. The important point is that there is not a single category in which we find a gender distinction in the plural. This is typologically quite a common pattern which is also found in languages such as Russian, Swedish and German.

Table 2: Morphological exponents of agreement in Somali

			SG	PL
VERBS	Present indicative	M	-aa	
				-aan
		F	-taa	
	Past indicative	M	-ay	
				-een
		F	-tay	
	Present subjunctive	M	-o	
				-aan
		F	-to	
PRONOUNS	Reduced personal	M	uu	
				ay
		F	ay	
	Full personal	M	isaga	
				iyaga
		F	iyada	
	Demonstrative	M	kan	
				kuwan
		F	tan	
	Possessive	M	-iis	
				-ood
		F	-eed	

The only reason to define a specific gender value for the plural form of nouns differing from the gender value in the singular is therefore to provide the means to correctly choose the appropriate definite article to be added to the noun itself in the plural.

If we consider how the gender value of a plural noun is established, there are various possibilities. Either the plural gender value is simply encoded in the lexicon alongside the singular gender value or it is established on the basis of the form of the definite article, the form of the plural suffix, or some other information about the noun, such as its singular gender and the form of the word's stem.

If the plural gender is encoded in the lexicon, this would mean that evident grammatical regularities are not captured in the grammar, but encoded in the lexicon as if plural gender were unpredictable. This would not be an economical way of describing Somali as it would load the lexicon and the speakers' memory with huge amounts of information that could easily be handled by a number of morphological rules.

If the plural gender value is instead established on the basis of the form of the plural definite article, and the sole purpose of ascribing a plural gender value is to predict the correct form of the definite article, we end up with circular reasoning: if we already know the definite form, we do not need the gender value to be able to generate this very form! Furthermore, the plural definite form would either have to be encoded in the lexicon or formed according to grammatical rules. Encoding the plural definite article in the lexicon would be just as uneconomical as encoding the plural gender.

Finally, if we assume that the plural gender can be deduced from other information present in the noun and that the purpose of ascribing the plural gender is solely to predict the correct form of the plural definite article, then the question arises as to why the plural definite article cannot instead be directly predicted based on the very information that is used in order to predict the plural gender. Why would we need to take this superfluous extra step via the gender value if we do not need the gender value for any other purpose?

Support for this point of view is also found in the typological literature. Elaborating the claim made by Hockett (1958: 231) that gender is 'reflected in the behavior of associated words', Corbett (2013: 89–90) states that the

> relevant 'reflection' in the associated words is agreement [...]. No amount of marking on a noun can prove that the language has a gender system; the evidence that nouns

have gender values in a given language lies in the agreement targets which show gender.

This is exactly the problem with the traditional description of plural gender in Somali. In the plural we do not find any trace of agreement in gender in other parts of speech, hence there is no reason to talk about gender in the plural. It is only in the singular that Somali exhibits gender agreement, and it is only this gender value that constitutes the necessary information to be encoded lexically in the noun. This gender value can be assumed to be stable, i.e. it may also be considered to be present in the plural. It will, however, not be referred to by any grammatical rule.

Therefore, I will instead argue that the form of the plural definite article may be in a straightforward manner predicted based on a noun's singular gender and its morphophonological characteristics. I will discuss in more detail the formation of the indefinite plural of nouns in Section 3 and then the choice of the definite plural article in Section 4.

3   The indefinite plural form of nouns

For the correct choice of the plural morpheme, the gender of the singular noun is crucial.

Regular feminine nouns fall into two main categories, as shown in Table 3. Those ending in -o in the singular will end in -ooyin in the plural, as in (a). Other nouns will add -o in the plural, as in (b–f). If the stem ends in -i, /y/ is inserted before the ending to avoid hiatus, as in (c). It should also be noted that a small number of nouns have a stem that differs from the singular surface form. The stem becomes evident in the plural, but because the stem ends in a consonant cluster, this stem-final cluster must be divided by an epenthetic vowel in the singular, as in (d). Most often the epenthetic vowel is a copy of the vowel in the root of the word, but there are individual exceptions, as in (e). Finally, stem-final /m/ or /k/ will be realised as /n/ and /g/ in the singular, as in (f), as Somali words may not end with /m/ or /k/.

Table 3: Examples of the plural formation of feminine nouns

(a)	hooyo	'mother'	hooyooyin
	dhalo	'bottle'	dhalooyin
(b)	kab	'shoe'	kabo
	kubbad	'ball'	kubbado
(c)	mindi	'knife'	mindiyo
	koofi	'hat'	koofiyo
(d)	gabadh	'girl'	gabdho
	dhibic	'drop'	dhibco
(e)	xubin	'bodypart'	xubno
(f)	maalin	'day'	maalmo

Regular masculine nouns fall into three main categories, as shown in Table 4.

Those ending in -e in the singular will end in -ayaal in the plural, as in (a). Those having only one syllable in the singular will form their plural by reduplication, which means that the last consonant of the stem is repeated after an intervening /a/, as in (b). Other masculine nouns will add -o in the plural, as in (c-h).

A small number of nouns have a stem that differs from the singular indefinite form. This is so because the stem ends with a consonant cluster. The stem becomes evident in the plural, but this stem-final cluster must be divided by an epenthetic vowel in the singular, as word-final clusters are not allowed in Somali. Such nouns simply add -o in the plural, as in (c). Most often the epenthetic vowel in the singular is simply a copy of the vowel in the root of the word, but there are individual exceptions, as in (d). Also, stem-final /m/ or /k/ will be realised as /n/ and /g/ in the singular, as in (e), because Somali words may not end with /m/ or /k/.

If instead the stem ends in a single consonant, the plural suffix will be reinforced. This reinforcement is realised in two different ways. In principle, if the final single consonant is b, d, l or n (m)[3] or r, this

---

[3]Somali syllables do not end in /m/. This means that /m/ that would be word-final is replaced by /n/, but when an ending is added to such a word, /m/

Table 4: Examples of the plural formation of masculine nouns

| (a) | aabbe | 'father' | aabbayaal |
| | fure | 'key' | furayaal |

(b)	miis	'table'	miisas
	bas	'bus'	basas
	qoys	'family'	qoysas
	dal	'country'	dalal

(c)	jilib	'knee'	jilbo
	xaraf	'letter of the alphabet'	xarfo
(d)	xarig	'rope'	xargo
(e)	ilig	'tooth'	ilko
(f)	aqal	'house'	aqallo
	albaab	'door'	albaabbo
	gambar	'stool'	gambarro
	xayawaan	'animal'	xayawaanno
(g)	dhinac	'side'	dhinacyo
	barnaamij	'programme'	barnaamijyo
	libaax	'lion'	libaaxyo
	yaxaas	'crocodile'	yaxaasyo
(h)	abti	'uncle (maternal)'	abtiyo[a]
	derbi	'wall'	derbiyo

[a] There is also a frequent, irregular form: abtiyaal.

consonant is doubled, as in (f), but if the final single consonant is another phoneme, /y/ is inserted between the stem and the plural -o, as in (g). Also, if the stem ends in the vowel -i, /y/ is inserted before the ending to avoid hiatus, as in (h).

As in practically every language, there are of course a small number of exceptions, some of which are listed in Table 5.

Certain exceptions form small groups, as in (a & b), whereas others are simply individual exceptions, as in (c & d).

The most prominent group of exceptions are some masculine nouns with only one syllable in the stem, which contains a long vowel. These

is able to reappear.

Table 5: Some examples of irregular plural formation

(a)	geed (M)	'tree'	geedo
	gees (M)	'horn'	geeso
	naas (M)	'breast'	naaso

(b)	wax (M)	'thing'	waxyaalo/waxyaabo
	si (F)	'manner'	siyaalo/siyaabo

(c)	walaal (M/F)	'sibling'	walaalo
(d)	buug (M)	'book'	buugaag

nouns exceptionally do not take the expected reduplication but simply add the suffix -o, as in (a), without any reinforcement of the stem-final single consonant.

4 The definite plural form of nouns

As shown in Section 2, Somali does not exhibit any gender agreement distinctions in the plural in any associated words. There is therefore no reason to define the gender of a noun in the plural. The form of the plural definite article is instead easily predictable on morphophonological grounds. The singular gender and the syllabic structure of the noun are enough to make the right choice.

All feminine plural nouns take the definite article {k}, as shown in Table 6.

It is realised as /k/ after the suffix -ooyin, as in (a), and as /h/ after the suffix -o, as in (b), while the plural suffix itself changes to /a/ as it is no longer word-final.

The choice of the plural definite article for masculine nouns depends mainly on the length of the noun, as shown in Table 7.

Indefinite masculine plural forms with only two syllables take the definite article {k}, which is realised in the same way as in the singular for nouns with reduplication, as in (a), and as /h/ after the suffix -o, which itself becomes /a/ as it is no longer word-final, as in (b).

Indefinite masculine plural forms with more than two syllables take the definite article {t}, which is realised as /d/ after the suffix

Table 6: Examples of the formation of the definite plural of feminine nouns

(a)	hooyooyin	'mothers'	hooyooyinka
	dhalooyin	'bottles'	dhalooyinka
(b)	kabo	'shoes'	kabaha
	kubbado	'balls'	kubbadaha
	mindiyo	'knives'	mindiyaha
	gabdho	'girls'	gabdhaha
	xubno	'body parts'	xubnaha
	maalmo	'days'	maalmaha

-o, which itself becomes /a/, as in (c), whereas it is realised as /ʃ/ after the suffix -yaal, leading to the loss of the preceding /l/, as in (d).

As can be expected, there are some exceptions, some of which are listed in Table 8.

In particular, there is a small group of monosyllabic masculine nouns with a long vowel in the root and a stem ending in /l/. As expected, they form their plural by reduplication. These nouns, however, take the definite article {t}, which is realised as /ʃ/, as in (a), possibly under the influence of the very large group of words with the suffix -ayaal, exemplified under (d) in Table 7.

Hence, the main principles for the choice of the plural definite article are as follows: (1) feminine nouns take the definite article {k} in the plural, (2) masculine nouns take the definite article {k} in the plural if the indefinite plural form contains only two syllables, whereas (3) longer masculine nouns take the definite article {t} in the plural.

Therefore, instead of the traditional view, referred to as GENDER POLARITY, presented above in Table 1, I propose a simpler interpretation of the definite articles and the gender system, as shown in Table 9. This analysis of the Somali gender system and its morphological exponents of definiteness is typologically uncontroversial. The notion of polarity may of course still be applied, but if so, only in order to

Table 7: Examples of the formation of the definite plural of masculine nouns

(a)	miisas	'tables'	miisaska
	basas	'buses'	basaska
	qoysas	'families'	qoysaska
	dalal	'countries'	dalalka
(b)	geedo	'trees'	geedaha
	geeso	'horns'	geesaha
	naaso	'breasts'	naasaha
	jilbo	'knees'	jilbaha
(c)	aqallo	'houses'	aqallada
	albaabbo	'doors'	albaabbada
	saaxiibbo	'friends'	saaxiibbada
	yaxaasyo	'crocodiles'	yaxaasyada
(d)	aabbayaal	'fathers'	aabbayaasha
	furayaal	'keys'	furayaasha

refer to the morphological exponents of definiteness.[4]

5   Singular or plural?

In textbooks and reference grammars of Somali there is sometimes slight variation with regard to whether certain forms are treated as singular or plural. The general obstacle is obviously the fact that there may at times be a difference between a word's form and its meaning, i.e. between the grammatical number and the number of persons or objects that the form refers to.

In order to avoid such confusion, the grammatical number of a word, i.e. whether the word should be treated as grammatically sin-

---

[4]Already when the concept of gender polarity was newly coined, Speiser (1938) objected to this idea when he discussed the general interrelationship between feminine derivational morphology, collectivity and plurality in Afroasiatic languages in general, giving numerous examples from Arabic and Hebrew.

Table 8: Some examples of irregular formation of the definite plural
of nouns

(a)	wiilal	'boys'	wiilasha
	geelal	'herds of camels'	geelasha
	ceelal	'wells'	ceelasha
	baalal	'feathers, wings'	baalasha
	suulal	'thumbs'	suulasha
	buulal	'huts, nests'	buulasha
(b)	buugaag	'books'	buugaagta

Table 9: Polarity of the exponents of definiteness in Somali nouns

	SINGULAR	PLURAL
FEMININE	{t}	{k}
MASCULINE	{k}	{t}

gular or plural, should be based on purely grammatical criteria, not
on the meaning of the word. The most practical way of handling this
situation is to define the number of a noun on the basis of its form.
A noun is singular if it has no plural morpheme, and plural if it has
a plural morpheme.

As we shall see, there might however be some disagreement on the
possible nature of a plural morpheme. In particular, there are several
nouns with a collective form that has traditionally been interpreted
as a plural form. These will be discussed in 5.4.1 and 5.4.2. There
are also several nouns with an Arabic plural form with a somewhat
unclear status in Somali. These nouns will be discussed below in
5.4.3.

5.1   Countables and uncountables

Besides the distinction between the singular and plural forms of nouns, there is also an important distinction to be made between nouns that have both a singular and a plural form and those that do not have both of these forms. The nouns that have both forms are referred to as countable nouns, whereas the nouns with only one number are referred to as uncountable nouns.

5.2   Types of uncountables

In Somali nearly all uncountable nouns are singular nouns, but there are some exceptions.

5.2.1   Pluralia tantum

Two Somali nouns have a plural form but no singular form. That the forms are actually plurals is confirmed by their agreement patterns in verbs and pronouns. They always agree in the plural, as in 1.

(1)   Waxa ay tagtay meel *ay biyo* ku *jiraan*.
      She went to a place where there is water.

Also, the definite article would not be expected to be /h/ if the words were singular, as singular nouns ending in -o are feminine and take the definite article /d/. These kinds of plural uncountable nouns are typologically not unusual and are generally referred to as PLURALIA TANTUM.

Table 10: The two *pluria tantum* in Somali

biyo	'water'	biyaha
caano	'milk'	caanaha

Apart from these two nouns, there are two other words that often trigger plural agreement, namely wax 'something' and maxay 'what', as in 2.

(2) a. Ma dareentay in *ay wax* khaldan*yihiin*
        Did you feel that something was wrong?

  b. *Maxaa* aad u malaynaysaa in *ay* ku *dhaceen*
        waraabihii?
        What do you think happened to the hyena?

These words, however, lack a plural morpheme and they may also trigger agreement in the singular. This unexpected agreement is therefore best explained by the fact that in the above example both of these words function as pronouns, and not as nouns. Of course, there is also the noun **wax** 'thing' that will trigger the expected agreement in the singular.

5.2.2 Mass nouns

Many uncountable nouns, including the two *pluralia tantum* just mentioned, i.e. **biyo** 'water' and **caano** 'milk', denote a substance that cannot be directly counted with numerals such as two, three, four etc. Instead, they have to be measured with the help of different kinds of units of measurement, e.g. 'a kilo of ...', 'a litre of ...', 'a metre of ...', 'a bottle of ...', 'a box of ...', 'a package of ...'. Such nouns are referred to as MASS NOUNS. Some examples include **bur** 'flour', **bun** 'coffee', **saliid** 'oil', **ciid** 'sand' and **sonkor** 'sugar'. Verbs and pronouns which agree with a mass noun, other than **biyo** 'water' and **caano** 'milk', are always in the singular, as in 3.

(3) ...Haddii maalintii la cabbo hal qasac oo cabbitaan
     sonkortu ku *jirto* ...
     ... if every day you drink a can of soda in which there is sugar
     ...

5.2.3 Collective nouns

In many languages a certain variation can be observed in the agreement pattern of verbs and other words that refer to certain types of nouns. Sometimes the agreement is in the singular, sometimes in the plural. This type of variation occurs, for instance, in both English and Swedish with words such as 'the team', as shown in 4.

(4)   a. The team *is* friendly.

     b. The team *are* friendly.

Such variation is typologically interesting and motivates a distinction between two types of agreement, defined by Corbett (2000: 187) as SYNTACTIC agreement, which is determined by the grammatical form of a noun, and SEMANTIC agreement, which is determined by the semantic meaning of a noun. Typologically, there are certain types of nouns that typically trigger this kind of variation.

The most important type of nouns triggering this variation in agreement in a number of languages are COLLECTIVE NOUNS. Corbett (2000: 118–9) applies the term 'collective' to a noun to indicate that it is 'referring to a group of items considered together rather than a number of items considered individually. [...] The primary function of collectives is to specify the cohesion of a group'. Most of the Somali nouns exhibiting variation in their agreement patterns can be included in this category, e.g. **dad** 'people', **dhallinyaro** 'youngsters', **carruur** 'children', **lo'** 'cattle', **dhir** 'plants', **geelley** 'camel owners, camel drivers', **quraanjo** 'ants', **rag** 'men', **dumar** 'women' etc., for which agreement occurs both in the singular and the plural, as shown in 5.

(5)   a. Maxaa ay *carruurtu* ugu *tukataa* safafka dambe
       ee masaajidka?
      Why do children pray in the rear rows of the mosque?

     b. Maxaa ay arki *karaan carruurtu*?
      What can the children see?

The collective noun **carruur** 'children' is itself grammatically singular, as it has no plural ending. It may therefore trigger syntactic agreement in the singular, as in 5a, but more often it triggers semantic agreement in the plural, as in 5b. It is also an uncountable noun, as it only occurs in one number, the singular, without a corresponding plural form.

5.3   Types of countables

Countable nouns, i.e. nouns that have both a singular and a plural form, also fall into a few different categories with respect to their agreement patterns, and this may at times also cause uncertainty about their number values. More specifically, the singular form is sometimes mistaken for a plural form when it triggers semantic agreement in the plural.

5.3.1   Corporate nouns

The notion of collective nouns is often used in a very broad sense, regardless of whether a noun is countable or uncountable. However, in order to clearly distinguish between the relevant types of nouns in Somali, one should consider using the term 'collective' only when referring to uncountable nouns, and use another term for the type of countable nouns that are in some respects similar to the collective uncountables.

The nouns in question are called CORPORATE NOUNS by Corbett (2000: 188), and he defines them as 'nouns which are singular morphologically and (typically) have a normal plural and yet, when singular, may take plural agreement', i.e. the singular form of such nouns may trigger both syntactic agreement in the singular and semantic agreement in the plural. For example, in 6a we find the singular noun **qoyskiisu** 'his family' with the plural predicate verb **dhaqdaan** 'breed' and the plural subject pronoun **ay** 'they'. The verb and the pronoun could, however, just as well have been in the masculine singular, like the predicate verb **yahay** 'is' and the subject pronoun **uu** 'he, it' in 6b.

(6)   a.   **Faarax** *qoyskiisu* **waxa** *ay dhaqdaan* **geel.**
Faarax's family breeds camels.

    b.   *Qoyskiisu* **waxa** *uu* **ka kooban** *yahay* **shan ruux.**
His family consists of five persons.

Corporate nouns typically denote sets or groups of persons, animals or objects, and some further examples of such Somali nouns are found in Table 11.

Table 11: Somali corporate nouns

SG.INDEF		SG.DEF	PL.INDEF	PL.DEF
qoys	'family'	qoys-ka	qoys-as	qoysas-ka
koox	'group, team'	koox-da	koox-o	kooxa-ha
geel	'herd of camels'	geel-a[a]	geel-al	geela-sha

[a] This noun is unique in realising the definite article {k} as zero in the singular.

5.4 Combinations of the above categories

The above types of nouns also enter into different types of semantic relations with each other, so that there is sometimes both a noun with a regular plural form and a collective noun with more or less the same meaning.

5.4.1 Nouns with three forms

A number of nouns are traditionally claimed to express number merely by means of a change in gender. This group of nouns, which has been called 'the 5th declension' by Saeed (1993: 134), Saeed (1999: 61) and Orwin (1995: 48), includes for instance the word dibi 'ox'. The form díbiga 'the ox', with a penultimate tonal accent on the stem, is masculine singular, whereas the form dibída 'the oxen', with a final tonal accent on the stem, is traditionally considered feminine plural. However, with the form dibída 'the oxen', a variation can be observed in the agreement patterns with verbs. They may occur in the plural or in the feminine singular, as in 7.

(7)   a. *Dibidu* waa ay *daaqayaan.*
        The oxen are grazing.

     b. *Dibidu* waa ay *daaqaysaa.*
        The oxen are grazing.

In 7a, the noun dibidu 'the oxen' is followed by the predicate verb daaqayaan 'are grazing' in the plural, whereas it may equally well, as in 7b, be followed by the verb form daaqaysaa in the feminine singular. This variation in agreement between the plural and the singular has been taken as evidence that plural forms like dibída 'the oxen' must be feminine, as the singular agreement is in the feminine gender (Hetzron (1972: 259–60), Zwicky and Pullum (1983: 391–3), Lecarme (2002: 134–7)). The reason, however, for having singular verb agreement with a plural noun, as in 7b, is not made clear.

At the beginning of Section 5, I argued that nouns without an explicit plural morpheme should be considered singular, hence the question is whether the form dibída 'the oxen' is actually feminine singular or feminine plural. If it were plural, it would be difficult to explain the verb agreement in the feminine singular. However, if it is actually feminine singular, as predicted by the fact that it has no overt plural morpheme, it is natural that syntactic agreement may trigger the singular on verbs, whereas plural agreement can readily be explained as semantic agreement, as the meaning of the feminine singular collective form dibída 'the oxen' is the concept of several animals seen as a coherent group. A more detailed argumentation in favour of the standpoint that such feminine forms are not plurals, but instead feminine singular collective nouns, can be found in Nilsson (2016).

Puglielli and Ciise Mohamed Siyaad (1984: 82) also state that plurals of this type have been recategorised as collectives; however, despite this statement they refrain from actually treating these forms as singulars. Also Puglielli and Abdalla Omar Mansur (1999) treat such forms as plurals.

Finally, it is important to point out a fact that is often not made clear enough in the literature, namely that most of the nouns in the 5th declension also have a completely regular plural form with an overt plural morpheme, as shown in Table 12.

The feminine form without a plural morpheme is just one of two possible ways of expressing more or less the same semantic content.

The type of nouns found in the 5th declension is thus highly interesting, as these nouns exhibit a singular, a regular plural and a collective singular form based on the very same root. The number of such noun stems is just a couple of dozen, but interestingly enough some newer words, often not mentioned in the literature, have also found their way into this group, e.g. the Arabic loanword baabuur

Table 12: Somali nouns with both a plural and a collective form

	SINGULAR		PLURAL	
M	díbi-ga	'the ox'	dibi-yá-da	'the oxen'
F.COLL	dibí-da	'the oxen'		
M	baabúur-ka	'the car'	baabuur-rá-da	'the cars'
F.COLL	baabuúr-ta	'the cars'		
M	búug-ga	'the book'	buug-aág-ta[a]	'the books
F.COLL	buúg-ta	'the books'		
M	túug-ga	'the thief	tuug-á-da	'the thieves'
F.COLL	tuúg-ta	'the thieves		

[a] This irregular form is much more frequent than the regular buugágga.

'car', as well as the English loanword buug 'book'.

5.4.2 Suppletive collective forms

Many ordinary countable nouns with a singular and a plural form have a semantically corresponding collective noun based on a totally different root. A number of such nouns are listed in Table 13.

Table 13: Different lexemes for collective and individualising meanings

	SINGULAR		PLURAL	
F	naag-ta	'the woman'	naag-a-ha	'the women'
M.COLL	dumar-ka	'the women'		
M	nin-ka	'the man'	nim-an-ka	'the men'
M.COLL	rag-ga	'the men'		
M	wíil-ka	'the boy'	wiil-a-sha	'the boys'
F	gabadh-a	'the girl'	gabdh-a-ha	'the girls'
F.COLL	carruur-ta	'the children'		

5.4.3 Arabic plural forms

There are also many nouns that take Arabic plural forms and exhibit
the type of variation already mentioned in their agreement patterns,
i.e. they may trigger agreement in verbs and pronouns both in the
singular and in the plural, as shown in 8.

(8)   a. Warqadaha daawooyinka ee *dhakhaatiirtu qorto*...
           Prescriptions for medications that doctors write...

      b. ...daawooyinka *dhakhaatiirtu* u *qoraan* dadka
           bukaanka ah.
           ...medications that doctors prescribe to people who are
           ill.

Such forms include both nouns with an Arabic plural suffix, like
the form macallim-iin-ta 'the teachers', which is traditionally considered a feminine plural form of the masculine singular macallin-ka
'the teacher', and nouns with a so-called Arabic broken plural, e.g.
the form kutub-ta 'the books', which is traditionally considered a
feminine plural form of the masculine singular noun kitaab-ka 'the
book'.

This variation in agreement is also confirmed by Puglielli and
Ciise Mohamed Siyaad (1984: 86), but they refrain from calling these
forms collectives. However, in order to be able to account for the
variation in number agreement, I will argue that such feminine forms,
containing Arabic plural morphemes, do not behave like ordinary
plurals with an indigenous Somali plural morpheme. Instead, they
have often, but probably not always, been reinterpreted as collective
forms which are grammatically singular, based on the same type of
agreement variation as was discussed in 5.4.1 with regard to nouns
of the traditional 5th declension. Some further nouns with an Arabic
plural are shown in Table 14.

5.4.4 Nouns without a grammatical plural

Another group of Somali nouns do not form any plural form with an
overt plural morpheme. These nouns only have a singular form and a
corresponding collective form which may trigger agreement either in

Table 14: Typical forms of nouns exhibiting a borrowed Arabic plural

	SINGULAR		PLURAL	
M	kursi-ga	'the chair'	kursi-ya-da	'the chairs'
F.COLL	kuraas-ta	'the chairs'		
M	kitaab-ka	'the book'	kitaab-ba-da	'the books'
F.COLL	kutub-ta	'the books'		
M	dhakhtar-ka	'the book'	dakhtar-ra-da	'the doctors'
F.COLL	dhakhaatiir-ta	'the doctors'		

the plural or in the feminine singular, thus this form is best described as feminine singular, e.g. **beeraley** 'farmers'.

For nouns of this type, there has generally been less confusion about the number values in the available reference grammars and textbooks. I will however argue that nouns like **Soomaali**, traditionally included in the 5th declension, also belong to the group of nouns lacking a plural. Some of these nouns are listed in Table 15.

Table 15: Somali nouns with a collective but without a plural form

	SINGULAR		PLURAL
M	Soomaáli-ga	'the Somali'	—
F.COLL	Soomaalí-da	'the Somalis'	—
M	askari-ga	'the soldier'	—
F.COLL	askar-ta	'the soldiers'	—
M	beeraala-ha	'the farmer'	—
F.COLL	beeraley-da	'the farmers'	—

5.4.5 Singulatives

Finally, a very small number of nouns exhibit a collective form as their most basic form, and a singular form is then derived from the collective. Such a morphologically derived form is generally called a SINGULATIVE (Corbett, 2000: 19). The most typical noun of this kind is **haween** 'women', as shown in Table 16.

Table 16: A Somali noun with a derived singulative form

	SINGULAR		PLURAL
M.COLL	haween-ka	'the women'	
F.SGTV	haween-ey-da	'the woman'	—

6 Summary

In this article, it has been shown that Somali nouns need only have one gender value. In the singular, verbs and pronouns agree in gender with the gender value of the governing noun. In the plural, no such agreement exists in Somali: the gender of a noun does not play any specific role in the plural, hence there is no reason to assume a gender value in the plural that would differ from the gender value in the singular.

There are four different regular Somali plural morphemes for nouns:

1. -o is used with most words. Additional adjustments to the preceding stem or the insertion of /y/ are quite common, and these phenomena follow distinct morphophonological rules;

2. reduplication is used with masculine nouns that are monosyllabic in the singular;

3. -ooyin is used with feminine nouns that end in -o in the singular;

4. -ayaal is used with masculine nouns that end in -e in the singular.

There are two definite article suffixes: {k}, realised as /k/, /g/, /h/ or zero, and {t}, realised as /t/, /d/, /ḍ/ or /ʃ/. Feminine nouns take the definite article {t} in the singular and the definite article {k} in the plural, whereas masculine nouns take the definite article {k} in the singular, and the definite article {t} in the plural, if the indefinite plural form has more than two syllables. An indefinite masculine plural noun with only two syllables instead takes the plural

definite article {k}.
The notion of collective nouns, i.e. formally singular uncountable nouns that denote a coherent set or group of persons, animals or objects, e.g. **carruur** 'children', is extremely important for the description of Somali nouns, as nouns of this type may trigger either syntactic agreement in the singular with regard to verbs and pronouns, or semantic agreement in the plural. The same is also true for the corporate nouns, e.g. **qoys** 'family', which differ from the collective nouns mainly in the fact that corporate nouns have both a singular and a plural form in order to denote one or several sets of objects. Many nouns with Arabic plural morphemes behave in a similar way to the collective nouns, e.g. **kuraas** 'chairs' or **macallimiin** 'teachers', with regard to the agreement patterns of verbs and pronouns.

References

Alejnikov, S. (2012). Grammatičeskij spravočnik. In S. Alejnikov (Ed.), *Somalijsko-russkij slovar'*. *Eraykoobka soomaali-ruush ah*, pp. 373–399. Moscow.

Berchem, J. (2012). *Referenzgrammatik des Somali*. Norderstedt: Books on Demand.

Corbett, G. (2000). *Number*. Cambridge: Cambridge University Press.

Corbett, G. G. (2013). Gender typology. In G. G. Corbett (Ed.), *The Expression of Gender (The Expression of Cognitive Categories 6)*, pp. 87–130. Berlin: De Gruyter Mouton.

El-Solami-Mewis, C. (1988). On classifying somali nouns by their plural classes. In M. Bechaus-Gerst and F. Serzisko (Eds.), *Cushitic-Omotic: Papers from the International Symposium on Cushitic and Omotic Languages (Cologne, January 6–9, 1986)*, Hamburg, pp. 555–563. Helmut Buske Verlag.

Hetzron, R. (1972). Phonology in syntax. *Journal of Linguistics* 8(2), 251–265.

Hockett, C. (1958). *A Course in Modern Linguistics.* New York: Macmillan.

Lecarme, J. (2002). Gender "polarity": Theoretical aspects of somali nominal morphology. In P. Boucher (Ed.), *Many Morphologies,* pp. 109–141. Somerville: Cascadilla Press.

Maxamed X. Raabbi (1994). *Naxwaha Sifeyneed ee Afsoomaaliga: Ereyeynta.* No publisher.

Moreno, M. M. (1955). *Il somalo della Somalia: Grammatica e testi del Benadir, Darod e Dighil.* Rome: Istituto Poligrafico dello Stato.

Nilsson, M. (2016). Somali gender polarity revisited. In D. L. Payne, S. Pacchiarotti, and M. Bosire (Eds.), *Diversity in African Languages,* pp. 451–466. Berlin: Language Science Press.

Omer Haji Bile Aden (2009). *Mabaadi'da salaynta iyo kala dhigdhigga Afka Soomaaliga.* Stockholm: Warsan OHBA Publications.

Orwin, M. (1995). *Colloquial Somali.* London & New York: Routledge.

Puglielli, A. and Abdalla Omar Mansur (1999). *Barashada Naxwaha Af Soomaaliga.* London: HAAN Associates.

Puglielli, A. and Ciise Mohamed Siyaad (1984). La flessione del nome. In A. Puglielli (Ed.), *Aspetti morfologici, lessicali e della focalizzazione (Studi somali 5),* pp. 53–114. Rome: Ministero degli affari esteri.

Saeed, J. (1993). *Somali Reference Grammar.* Kensington, Maryland: Dunwoody Press.

Saeed, J. I. (1999). *Somali,* Volume 10 of *London Oriental and African Language Library.* Amsterdam: John Benjamins.

Speiser, E. (1938). The pitfalls of polarity. *Natural Language and Linguistic Theory 14*(3), 187–202.

Zwicky, A. and G. Pullum (1983). Phonology in syntax: The somali optional agreement rule. *Natural Language and Linguistic Theory 1*(3), 385–402.

The behaviour of the suffixes -le, -ley, -ey and la in Somali

Cabdiraxmaan C. Faarax 'Guri-Barwaaqo'

University of Hargeysa, hal_aqoon@yahoo.com

This article was originally written in Somali and was translated by Martin Orwin.

Abstract

Since the time the Latin alphabet was chosen to write Somali, Somali writers and experts have brought together their strengths in the collection of unwritten literature which has then been published. On the other hand, the work that foreign scholars working on Somali language were mostly concerned with, and still are mostly concerned with, is different. These scholars didn't so much anthologize literature rather they undertook to try to understand something of the syntax, the behaviour of the language and the rules which guide it. Be that as it may, it is appropriate that the two activities are undertaken and that a balance between them is found. Thus, in this short article, I shall present the behaviour of the suffixes -le, -ley, -ey and -la' found in Somali.

1 Behaviour of the suffix -le

I begin with the suffix -le. Firstly we can say that it is a syllable because it fulfils the requirements of the syllable which are that the sound is made up of a consonant and a vowel (long or short). Next it is an affix (**nudane**), specifically a suffix, which is added to the end of the noun. It is worth mentioning that the suffix can be described as having two contrasting meanings; that is the suffix -le sometimes brings a positive meaning and sometimes a negative one.

1.1 The positive meaning of the suffix -le

The suffix mentioned above, when it is positive expresses possession and derives from the word **leh** as in the examples in 1.

(1)

a. **adhiile**
   adhi+leh
   a person with sheep and goats or many sheep and goats

b. **baarwiille**
   baar+wiil+le
   a burden camel with hair on its hump like that on a boy's head

c. **bacadle**
   bacad+le
   a place with many un-covered pitches where goods are sold

d. **balligubadle**
   balli+gubad+le
   water reservoir+burned area+le
   a water storage place with burned land around it

e. **beyle**
   bey+le
   a person with the colour grey

f. **buuhoodle**
   buuhood+le
   marshy land with standing water+le
   a marshy place with standing water

g. **ceelberdaale**
   ceel+berde+le
   well+wild fig trees+le
   a place with wild fig trees

h. **faanoole**
   faano+le
   elephant tusk+le
   a place with many ele-phant tusks

i. **gadhle**
   gadh+le
   beard+le
   a man with a large beard

j. **geeddeeble**
   geed+deeb+le
   tree+wood ash+le
   a tree with wood ash

k. **geelle**
   geel+le
   camels+le
   a man with many camels

l. **godadle**
   godad+le
   holes+le
   a man who has rela-tionships with many women

m. hariiryaale
hariiryo+le
type of grass mat+le
with **hariiryo** grass
mats

n. hiiraale
hiiro+le
receding hair+le
a man with receding
hair

o. marqaale
marqo+le
a tree on which peo-
ple put small pieces
of cloth as they
pass+le[1]

p. qoob adhiile
qoob+adhi+le
hooves+sheep and

goats+le
a person with many
sheep and goats

q. riyoole
riyo+le
goats+le
a person with many
goats

r. sugulle
sugul+le
the colour of char-
coal+le
a person the colour of
charcoal

s. waranle
waran+le
spear+le
a spear-bearer (war-
rior)

1.2 Other positive meanings of -le

When it is positive, the suffix -le can also express a trade or craft
as in 2. Note that when words end in '-o' or '-i' these lengthen to
'-oo' and '-ii' when -le or -ley is added as shown in the examples.

(2) a. biyoole
biyo+le
water+le
a man who sells water

b. caanoole
caano+le

milk+le
a man who sells milk

c. dawaarle
dawaar+le
sewing machine+le
a male tailor

---

[1]The original meaning of **marqo** is 'cover over a camel's udders to prevent
suckling'. I have not been able to find out how this relates to the meaning of
marqaale.

d. dhuxulle
dhuxul+le
charcoal+le
a man who sells or
trades charcoal

e. doobbiile
doobbi+le
laundry+le
a person with a laun-
dry

f. harqaanle
harqaan+le
sewing machine+le
a male tailor

g. qaadle
qaad+le
khat+le
a man who sells khat

h. roodhiile
roodhi+le
bread+le
a man who makes
and/or sells bread

i. rinjiile
rinji+le
paint+le
a painter and decora-
tor

1.3 The suffix -le when it is negative

When the suffix -le is negative it expresses lack of something such
as in 3.

(3) a. cagoole
cago+le
feet/legs+le
a person disabled in
walking

b. candhoole
candho+le
udders+le
a she-camel that can-
not produce milk

c. dhegoole
dhego+le
ears+le
a deaf person

d. dhuule
dhuu+le

jacket made of
hide+le
a person born not
having a hide garment
to wear

e. faroole
faro+le
fingers+le
a person missing some
or all fingers

f. feedhoole
feedho+le
ribs+le
a person missing ribs
i.e. a thin, skinny
person

g. ilkoole
ilko+le
teeth+le
a person missing some
or all teeth

h. indhoole
indho+le

eyes+le
a blind person

i. lugoole
lugo+le
legs+le
a person missing one
or both legs

2 Behaviour of the suffix -ley

The suffix -ley, like the suffix -le, when it is positive sometimes
expresses possession as in 4.

(4) a. cadaadley
cadaad+ley
thorn tree species+ley
a place where there
are cadaad thorn
trees

b. dacawaley
dacawo+ley
jackals+ley
a place where there
are many jackals

c. dameeraley
dameero+ley
donkeys+ley
a place where there
are many donkeys

d. foodley
food+ley
young girl's hairstyle
at the front of the
head +ley
a girl with the food

hairstyle

e. gabiiley
gabiyo+ley
cliffs+ley
a place with cliffs

f. qoolley
qool+ley
ring around the
neck+ley
a bird with a ringed
neck

g. qoryooley
qoryo+ley
firewood+ley
a place with firewood

h. qudhacley
qudhac+ley
thorn tree+ley
a place with thorn
trees

i. quruuruxley
quruurux+ley

pebbles+ley
a place with pebbles

j. sallaxley
sallax+ley
smooth rocks+ley
a place with smooth

rocks

k. caraancarley
caraancar+ley
thistle-like plants+ley
a place with thistle-
like plants

The suffix -ley at other times expresses the work a person has, specifically women, as in 5.

(5)   a. biyooley
biyo+ley
water+ley
a woman who sells
water

b. caanaley
caano+ley
milk+ley
a woman who sells or
trades milk

c. dawaarley
dawaar+ley

sewing machine+ley
a woman tailor

d. harqaanley
harqaan+ley
sewing machine+ley
a woman tailor

e. qaadley
qaad+ley
khat+ley
a woman who trades
khat

3   Assimilation of 'l' to 'r'

When the noun ends in 'r', the 'l' of the suffixes -le and -ley may change to 'r' as in 6.

(6)   a. dawaarre
dawaar+le
see 2c

b. garre
gar+le
when 'dh' is pro-
nounced as 'r', see 1i

c. barre
bar+le
speckles, freckles+le
a person with specks
or freckles on their
skin

d. dawaarrey
dawaar+ley

see 5c

e. dhoorrey
dhoor+ley
child's haircut with a
crest down the mid-
dle+ley

a child with a **dhoor**
haircut

f. caraancarrey
caraancar+ley
see 4k

4 Behaviour of the suffix -ey

The suffix -ey in its own way displays similar interesting behaviour.
Sometimes the behaviour is positive and sometimes negative. When
it is positive it expresses possession as in 7. Note that when the noun
ends in 'x', -ey becomes -ay as in 7c and 7d.

(7) a. calooley
calool+ey
stomach/belly+ey
a person with a large
belly

b. dhoobey
dhoob+ey
mud+ey
a place with a lot of
mud

c. madaxay
madax+ey
head+ey
a person with a large
head

d. qorraxay
qorrax+ey
clear sun+ey
a place with clear sun

e. xundubey
xundub+ey
umbilical hernia+ey
a person with an um-
bilical hernia

f. uurey
uur+ey
pregnancy+ey
a woman with a large
pregnancy

When the suffix is negative it expresses lack of something as in 8.

(8) a. gacaney
gacan+ey
hand+ey
a person without a

hand or with an in-
jury to a hand

b. ganey
gan+ey

broken front tooth+ey
a person with a broken front tooth

c. iley
il+ey
eye+ey
a person without an eye or who has something wrong with an eye

d. iligey
ilig+ey

tooth+ey
a person without a tooth or with a broken tooth

e. xiirey
xiir+ey
shaven head+ey
a person with a shaven head or with no hair

5 The suffix -la and its behaviour

The word la' is grammatically an adjective meaning 'lacking', for example: qof indho la' 'a person who is lacking eyes (a blind person)'. In a manner similar to the word leh losing the final consonant when it becomes a suffix and is added to a noun, la' loses the final glottal stop (') as in the examples in 9. Thus, qof ceeb la' means 'a person lacking shameful behaviour (ceeb)', referring to that person's behaviour. However, Waxaan arkay Ceebla means 'I saw Ceebla (a woman called Ceebla)'. In an analogous manner, when la' loses the glottal stop and becomes a suffix on the words cawro, midhif and saxar they become proper names as in 9. Example 9g is a masculine example.

(9)   a. cawro la'
cawro+la'
parts of the body which are covered (here implying ugliness)
a person without ugliness

b. Cawrala
cawro+la
ugliness+la
proper name with meaning as in 9a

c. midhif la'
midhif+la'

small-droppings or bits of debris+la'
a person without small droppings or bits of debris, here implying a lack of anything to disapprove of

d. Midhifla
midhif+la

small droppings or bits of debris+la
proper name with meaning as in 9c

e. carrab la'
carrab+la'

tongue+la'
a person without a tongue (a person who lisps)

f. Carrabla
carrab+la

tongue+la
proper name with meaning as in 9e

g. Carrablow
carrab+low

tongue+low
lit: a man without a tongue (a man who lisps)

6 Conclusion

In this short article I have looked at the behaviour of the suffixes -le, -ley, -ey and -la. I have described them as having positive and negative meanings when they are suffixed to different nouns. For example the suffix -le sometimes expresses possession as in 1 and at other times it expresses trade or craft such as in 2. At other times it expresses the lack of something as in 3. The other suffixes -ey and -ley behave in an analogous manner. I also described how the word la' loses the glottal stop when it goes with some nouns and gives to some a positive and to some a negative meaning.

The Pharyngeal Loss and V-raising in Oromo

Mohamed Diriye Abdullahi

Independent scholar, Hargeysa
mdiriye@hotmail.com

Abstract

This article considers the direction of change and the cause of the loss of the pharyngeals in what are here termed Oromoid languages, specifically Oromo and Maay. The lack of pharyngeals is considered in relation to Somali. It is suggested that this is related to vowel raising.

1   Introduction

If the Oromoid languages had lost pharyngeals, the question is what is the direction of the change or what caused the change? The term 'Oromoid', in this case, refers to languages without pharyngeals such as Oromo and Maay. The former is well known and needs no introduction but the latter is usually less known and has been classified, wrongly I believe, as a dialect of Somali. In the following discussion, a directional change rule is proposed to explain how Oromo and Maay lost the pharyngeals.

Oromoid languages have no pharyngeals (ħ and ʕ) (x and c in the Somali alphabet). The Somali ʕ correponds to zero, usually; while the Somali ħ corresponds to [h] in Oromo and Maay.

V-raising   Before we attempt to formulate a rule for pharyngeal loss, we could present a rule that seems to operate in Oromo and Maay when contrasted with Somali. We will call it the rule of V-raising for Oromo and Maay (see 1).

(1)   V [-high] → V [+high] / _ C [-sonorant]

The rule simply states that the low vowels in Somali correspond to high vowels in the Oromo and Maay reflexes. Examples from Maay are given in Table 1, but the same is true also for Oromo.

Table 1:

Somali	Maay	
madaħ	mete	'head'
adi	edi	'you'
ari	eri / erin	'sheep'
ʕaws	ees	'grass'
gurbaʕ	gurbi	'a young male camel in Somali / a male camel in Maay'
tusbaħ	usbi	'rosary'

But this isn't apparent in the opposite direction as shown in Table 2:

Table 2:

gaal (Maay)	*geel (c.f. Somali geel)	'camel / herd of camels'
gana (Oromo)	*gena	'hand'
gaas (Maay)	*gees	'horn'

However, we must be cautious, just as Grimm (cited in Goyvaerts, 1975: p.37) cautioned that his 'sound shift' rule, known today as Grimm's rule in Indo-European studies was not to be taken as systematically absolute, that the rule in 1 is not absolute but is rather a general trend.

Pharyngeal loss   Now we can turn to the second part—pharyngeal loss—which at once seems to be related to V-raising. Table 3 shows the features which I suggest the pharyngeals in Somali share and don't share with their reflexes in Oromo and Maay.

Table 3:

	Pharyngeals (Somali) ʕ, ħ	Reflexes (Oromo & Maay) ʔ, h
Features	-high	+high
	+back	+back
	-sonorant	+sonorant

We note that a similar relationship exists between the high and low vowels as shown in Table 4.

Table 4:

	Low vowel a	High vowel i
Features	-high	+high

The glottals (on the right side of Table 1) are technically +high, and +back—the jaw is not lowered—and they are, anyway, at the back of the vocal tract. This is not usually specified in textbooks, but as far as Cushitic is concerned, they appear to function as +high and +back, and we can take that as being part of the vocalic processes. In other words, pharyngeals are -high, whereas glottals +high.

To further simplify the validity of this matter, we tried an experiment trying to pronounce some words with pharyngeals without lowering our jaw. These were the Somali words containing pharyngeals: [ħ]idid (xidid) 'root' and [ʕeːb] (ceeb) 'shame'.

It was difficult, and what we were vocalizing was nearer to the glottals than to the pharyngeals. We were thus vocalizing essentially: [h]idid and [eːb].

To return to the phonetic discussion, it appears that pharyngeals were equivalently replaced through the rule in 2.

(2)   ħ [-sonorant, -high, -voice] → h [+sonorant, +high, -voice]

The feature +high is not a feature usually associated with /h/, the glottal fricative, but in this context, we can say it is the opposite of ħ. Let us discount the +voice feature, since this is redundant (a

+sonorant consonant is also +voice). Let us also disregard the -voice feature on the pharyngeal side. So what we have is given in Rule 3.

(3) C [-sonorant, -high] → ʔ [+sonorant, +high]

If simplified even more, we can say what is given in 4.

(4) obstruent → +sonorant (weakening)

The rule in 3 says simply that low obstruents [-sonorant, -high] were raised. Since the only obstruents which are [-sonorant, -high] are ħ and ʕ, these were replaced homorganically.

But ʕ has no corresponding sonorant that can be mapped, thus it is replaced with a segment having [+sonorant, +high, +back, +voice] features. The only possibilities are /a/ or /w/, which are [+sonorant, +high, +back, +voice]. Since these are syllabic elements, the replacement is usually zero. The desired segment is too vowel-like and is usually just deleted (see Table 5).

Table 5:

Somali	Maay, Oromo	
ʕaːno	wan (Maay), aanan (Oromo)	'milk'
ʕaws	ees	'grass'

Whereas, ħ [-sonorant, -high, -voice] is replaced with [+sonorant, +high, -voice], which is h as in the example in Table 6.

Table 6:

Somali	Maay	
ħidid	hidid	'root'

The Cause for Change Pharyngeals are the only +low obstruents in the Cushitic system. Thus, when the vowels were raised to /e/ or /i/, the +high feature of the vowel spread over to them, since more and more of the vowel segments were now converted to +high. This raises the question of a causal factor that started the chain of changes.

We do not know of a definitive causal factor, which can be either internal or external. However, one may well note the process seems to be one of lenition; one may also note that the change occurs from low vowels that demand more energy to high vowels that demand less energy. Furthermore, one may note that pharyngeals have high energy demand as [-sonorant, -high, +back] whereas the replacing counterparts do not. Now, whether this is a pristine manifestation of the economy principle (Martinet, 1961) or not is a debatable question.

For an example of an external motivating factor, we have to go back to contact phenomena. It is known that the Oromo and other allied groups came into contact by way of conquest with Nilotic and Bantu peoples, whose languages lack the pharyngeals, possibly influencing and being influenced in the process.

Bibliography

Goyvaerts, D. (1975). *Present-day Historical and Comparative Linguistics*. Ghent, Antwerp: E. Storia Scientia.

Martinet, A. (1961). *Eléments de linguistique générale*. Paris: Armand Colin.

A Platform for a Bilingual French-Somali Dictionary

Moubarak Ahmed Mohamoud

Institut des Langues de Djibouti, Centre d'Etudes et de Recherche de Djibouti
moubanov@hotmail.com

Abstract

ABSTRACT NEEDED

1 Introduction

Already as an ancient part of the written tradition of language we find the first traces of lexicography in glossaries and word lists. In the Greek world it comprised, for example, comments on the meaning of rare words or technical terms such as the lexicon produced by the school of Abdera on the work of Homer. In the sixteenth and seventeenth centuries, the first bilingual dictionaries were published in Europe, e.g. *A Dictionarie French and English: published for the benefite of the studious in that language* by the Huguenot, Claude de Sainliens or *A Dictionarie of the French and English Tongues* by the famous English lexicographer Randle Cotgrave.

In its contemporary definition, lexicography is positioned as 'the technique of making dictionaries and the linguistic analysis of this technique' (Dubois et al., 1973). It is, however, a very recent discipline for the languages of some societies, in particular for African languages.

Early lexicographical contributions in Africa were made in the 1800s by missionaries and colonial administrators. In their concern for evangelization and communication with the people of Africa, they produced several works of a lexicographical nature. Although they gradually improved, these works only managed to meet metalexicographical criteria (methods used for compiling dictionaries) and the semantics, syntax or pragmatics were neglected in these dictionaries. Moreover, the dictionaries compiled by missionaries and colonial administrators were mostly bilingual dictionaries.

Somali is no exception to this phenomenon. Developing just as well as other languages in Africa, the first traces of Somali lexicography date back to the late nineteenth century with a more pronounced development in the twentieth century. We can mention, for example, the *Wörterbuch Somali-Deutsch* published in 1902 by L. Reinisch with about 8,500 entries, the *Dizionario della lingua Somala* published in 1915 by De Palermo with 7,000 entries and also the *Somali-English Dictionary* written by R.C. Abraham published in 1964 and his *English-Somali Dictionary* published in 1967 (both published by University of London Press).

This period marks the birth of a Somali lexicographical culture, and many bilingual dictionaries were published during the period preceding the introduction of the official writing system of this Cushitic language. It was in 1972 that Somali became 'a national language with an official writing system' (Puglielli, 2015: p.61). As soon as the orthography was established, the need to develop a monolingual Somali dictionary arose. The revolutionary government immediately gave this difficult task to a committee chaired by Yaasiin Cismaan Keenadiid. Their famous *Qaamuuska Af-Soomaaliga* 'Dictionary of the Somali language' was published by Wasaaradda Hiddaha Taclinta Sare, Akademiyaha Dhaqanka Guddiga Af-Soomaaliga in 1976. The publication of this dictionary 'for its simplicity and its clarity, was the starting point of several bilingual or trilingual dictionaries around the world'. (Idris Youssouf Elmi, 2007: p.81)

As for the Republic of Djibouti, it has also seen a lexicographical history dating from the colonial era. The first known dictionary is the *Essai de vocabulaire pratique français-issa (Somalis) avec prononciation figurée*, which was published in 1897 by Léon Henry. Fifteen years later, the *Dictionnaire français-arabe des dialectes parlés à Djibouti et dans les pays environnants Dankali, Somali, au Yemen et à Aden* by Laurent Depui was published in 1912. It was followed by Hoffmann's *Dictionnaire de la langue somalie* consisting of two volumes (French-Somali / Somali-French) published in 1960. In 1986, the *Manuel de conversation Somali-Français* of Véronique Carton-Dibeth was published by L'Harmattan. It also deserves mentioning that 'more than two decades after the second monolingual publication, the Republic of Djibouti and its Institute of Languages' (Idris Youssouf Elmi, 2007: p.81) published *Ileeye*, the dictionary of Saalax Xaashi Carab in 2004. Then comes the publication of *Soo Maal*, the monolingual dictionary of 70,000 entries published by the Institut des Langues de Djibouti (ILD) and Somali Pen International on the occasion of the 40th anniversary celebrations of the Somali orthography, which took place in Djibouti in December 2012. The latest lexicographical project underway is the FranSom project.

2 The FranSom Project

FranSom is an ongoing project involving the development of a bilingual dictionary French–Somali. It involves four institutions: the Université de Djibouti, Institut des Langues de Djibouti, Università degli studi di Napoli "L'Orientale" and the Resdsea Cultural Foundation.

The project is threefold with the first aim being to make up for the lack of a true bilingual French–Somali dictionary that meets the standards of modern lexicography. It should be noted that a dictionary 'is not just a simple colletion of words; an adequate description of the lexicon of a language implies the knowledge of the whole system of the language in object. This is because a language is a coherent system where different levels of organization interact (from phonology to text/discourse), and because when we speak we do not use single words but sentences (i.e. combinations of them).' (Puglielli, 2015: p.61). To show some shortcomings of these types of dictionaries, let us consider, for example, a few entries in the *Dictionnaire FRANCAIS-SOMAL* BY Abdulghani Gourré Farah published in 2008 shown in Figure 1.

Figure 1: Extract from Abdulghani Gourré Farah's dictionary

ACCOMPAGNER [aakoonpaanyee] v. raacid, wehelin.

ACCOMPLIR [aakoonpliir] v. samayn, dhammayn. - Accomplir un devoir: samayn, dhammayn waajib ku saarnaa.

ACCORD [aakoor] n.m. heshiis.

ACCORDÉON [aakoordeyoo'n] n.m. qalab muusikeed sida makiinadda teebka meel faraha lagu garaaco leh.

ACCORDER [aakoordee] v. 1. yeelid. 2. heshiin.

This resembles more a glossary than a dictionary. A dictionary has been defined as:

> a cultural object that has the lexicon of one (or more) languages in alphabetical order, providing for each entry a number of pieces of information (pronunciation, etymology, part of speech, definition, construction, examples of use, synonyms, idioms); this information is needed to allow the translation from one language to another or to fill gaps that do not allow him to understand a text in its original language

(Dubois et al. (1973))

As for a glossary, this was originally a collection of 'glosses', that is to say a limited number of obscure words or technical terms that the author seeks to define and which led to glossaries of medicine, glossaries of art, war, etc. Today the term means to 'index a speaker' (often of a dialect or an understudied language) or the vocabulary of a scientific or technical field.

Another major aim is that since the Somali language has an oral tradition and an offical orthography was only introduced in 1972, the absence of an effective standardization is related 'to the fact that the central institution which had been in charge of its standardization collapsed with the central government of Somalia in 1992' (Banti and Ismaïl, 2015: p.45). The second aim therefore of the FranSom project is to strengthen standardization of the language.

Finally, the third major aim of this dictionary will be to develop an essential tool for the possible teaching of Somali in Djibouti. Djibouti is a republic in which Arabic and French are official languages. The latter is, at once, the language of administration and the medium *par excellence* of education in Djibouti at the expense of Somali and Afar, which, although they have the status of national languages, have never been taught in schools. However there is a will on the part of the government for the introduction of the teaching of these two national languages in the education system of the country.

Like any dictionary of this size, it has a wide and diverse readership. It is aimed, first of all, at students and teachers, but in general, to any Somali-speaking person wishing to learn French. The immediate objective of the project is to translate the 4000 most used words of the French language with a longer term goal of 10,000 words in future editions of the dictionary. The selection of these words was made using a statistical method based on word frequency in the language determined from a corpus of hundreds of thousands of texts. The first issue of the dictionary will be prepared online and an electronic version (available for computer and smartphone) will appear prior to its print publication.

3 The platform

The development of a dictionary necessarily requires the use of computer tools to facilitate the tasks of lexicographers. To this end, several types of software for the management of textual databases exist. Among these is Toolbox, which is the successor of the older Shoebox. Toolbox can support the production of bilingual or trilingual dictionaries.

The FranSom team began to work with this programme during the first year. Some time later, however, the flaws of this tool became evident and delayed the work of the various parties involved in the project. Among the limitations of the system was, for example, the lack of ability to coordinate easily between the different editors working in four different countries (France, Italy, Djibouti and Somaliland). There was also difficulty in converting the database to other formats and a flaw in the security system that could allow any malicious user to break into the system to retrieve files remotely.

Given these problems, a new, one-off platform was set up exclusively for the project. This has greatly facilitated the work and has particularly enabled each person to work on their own while still collaborating. Among other benefits of this platform are:

- it respects the spelling of French as well as that of Somali;

- easy file conversion to PDF, Word and other formats;

- the presence of Dictionnaire FRANCAIS-SOMAL by Abdulghani Gourré Farah as well as, for a large number of entries, a translation into English and Italian (this facilitates the search for the word in various other bilingual dictionaries).

To access the system an internet connection is needed which allows the work to be done with confidence and for the work done by each of the team members to be followed by the others. Each editor enters the system with a unique user ID and password as shown in Figure 2.

Figure 2: Initial entry page into the FranSom platform

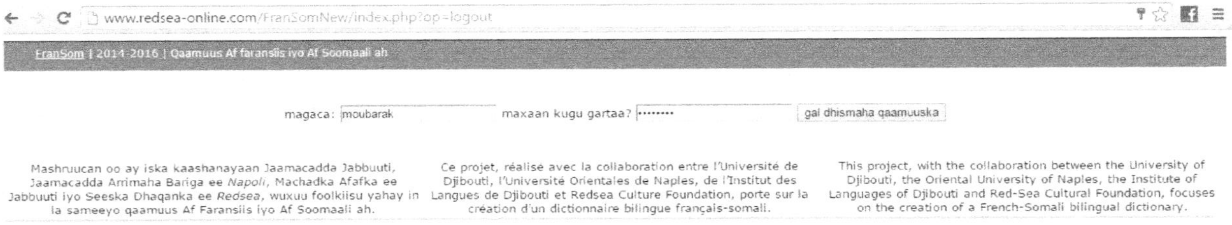

www.redsea-online.com/FranSomNew/index.php?op=logout
FranSom | 2014-2016 | Qaamuus Af faransiis iyo Af Soomaali ah
magaca: moubarak
maxaan kugu gartaa?
gal dhismaha qaamuuska
Mashruucan oo ay iska kaashanayaan Jaamacadda Jabbuuti, Jaamacadda Arrimaha Bariga ee Napoli, Machadka Afafka ee Jabbuuti iyo Seeska Dhaqanka ee Redsea, wuxuu foolkiisu yahay in la sameeyo qaamuus Af Faransiis iyo Af Soomaali ah.
Ce projet, réalisé avec la collaboration entre l'Université de Djibouti, l'Université Orientales de Naples, de l'Institut des Langues de Djibouti et Redsea Culture Foundation, porte sur la création d'un dictionnaire bilingue français-somali.
This project, with the collaboration between the University of Djibouti, the Oriental University of Naples, the Institute of Languages of Djibouti and Red-Sea Cultural Foundation, focuses on the creation of a French-Somali bilingual dictionary.

Figure 3: Alphabetical list of entries page

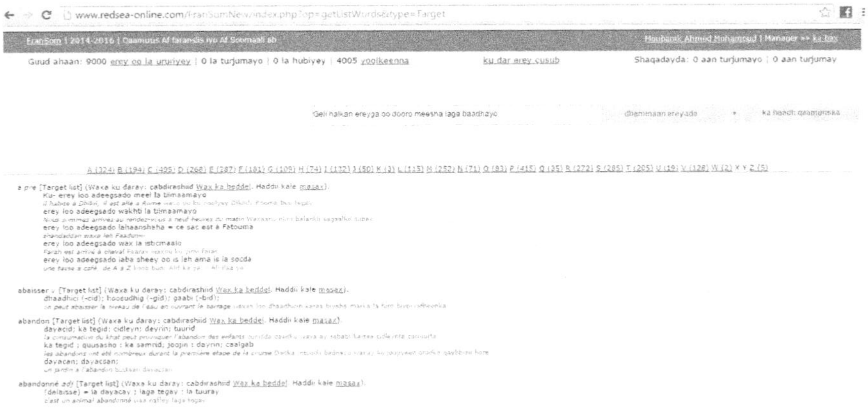

www.redsea-online.com/FranSomNew/index.php?op=getListWords&type=Target
FranSom | 2014-2016 | Qaamuus Af faransiis iyo Af Soomaali ah
Guud ahaan: 9000 erey oo la ururiyey | 0 la turjumayo | 0 la hubiyey | 4005 yoolkeenna
ku dar erey cusub
Shaqadayda: 0 aan turjumayo | 0 aan turjumay

Once logged in, the link '4000 yoolkeenna' gives a list of all entries sorted alphabetically and a page is displayed as shown in Figure 3.

In order to work on any entry, the link 'Wax ka beddel', located on the right, allows work on any entry via the window shown in Figure 4.

Figure 4: Page for editing entries

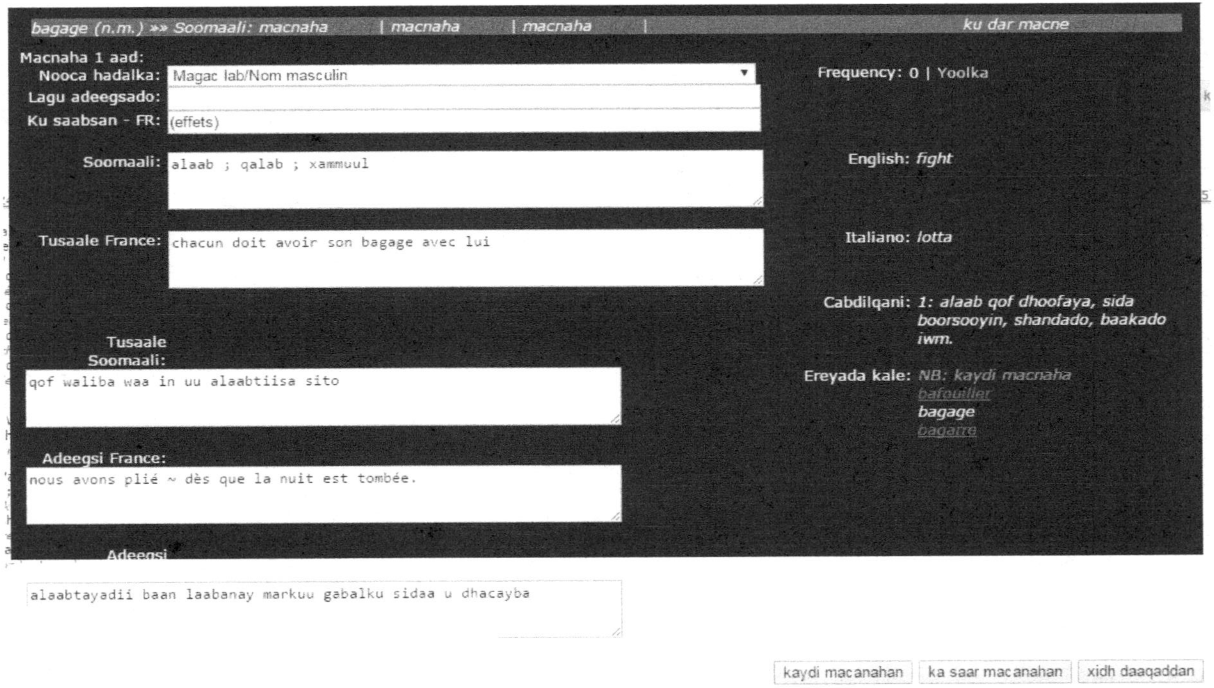

bagage (n.m.) »» Soomaali: macnaha | macnaha | macnaha | ku dar macne

Macnaha 1 aad:
Nooca hadalka: Magac lab/Nom masculin   Frequency: 0 | Yoolka
Lagu adeegsado:
Ku saabsan - FR: (effets)

Soomaali: alaab ; qalab ; xammuul   English: *fight*

Tusaale France: chacun doit avoir son bagage avec lui   Italiano: *lotta*

                                                           Cabdiqani: **1: alaab qof dhoofaya, sida boorsooyin, shandado, baakado iwm.**

                                                           Ereyada kale: *NB: kaydi macnaha*
Tusaale   *bafouillat*
Soomaali: **bagage**
qof waliba waa in uu alaabtiisa sito   *bagarre*

Adeegsi France:
nous avons plié ~ dès que la nuit est tombée.

        Adeeqsi

alaabtayadii baan laabanay markuu gabalku sidaa u dhacayba

                                                           kaydi macanahan   ka saar macanahan   xidh daaqaddan

As can be seen in the top row, there are small boxes for each meaning of an entry. For example, by clicking on 'macnaha 1aad' (first meaning), for each and every entry what needs to be indicated are its grammatical category and features (verb, masculine or feminine, adjective, adverb, preposition, etc.) and its lexical field (if it is specific to a certain domain, for example medicine, music, military etc.). Then the word's definition is given in French and translated into Somali. Following these are fields for examples in French and their translation into Somali. Finally, if there are any common expressions, any proverbs or sayings etc. in which the word is used, they are mentioned under 'Adeegsi France' and then translated under 'Adeegsi Somali'. Once completed, the button 'kaydi macnahan' saves the changes and the window is closed with 'xidh daaqaddan' which leads to the editing changes page shown in Figure 5.

Figure 5: Page showing editing changes

à pre [Target list] (Waxa ku daray: cabdirashiid Wax ka beddel. Haddii kale masax).
Ku- erey loo adeegsado meel la tilmaamayo
il habite à Dhikil; il est allé à Rome waxa uu ku noolyay Dikhil; Rooma buu tegey
erey loo adeegsado wakhti la tilmaamayo
Nous sommes arrivés au rendez-vous à neuf heures du matin Waxaanu nimi balankii sagaa
erey loo adeegsado lahaanshaha = ce sac est à Fatouma
shandaddan waxa leh Faadumo
erey loo adeegsado wax la isticmaalo
Farah est arrivé à cheval Faarax waxuu ku yimi faras
erey loo adeegsado laba sheey oo is leh ama is la socda
une tasse à café; de A à Z koob bun; Alif ka ya' - Ali ilaa ya'

In conclusion this platform is an innovation in dictionary-making techniques. It is incredibly useful for our work and has helped us greatly in organizing and harmonizing our various contributions by allowing us to work more closely with each other.

Bibliography

Banti, G. and A. M. Ismaïl (2015). Some issues in somali orthography. In C. C. M. Cabdirashid M. Ismaaciil and S. A. Sharci (Eds.), *Afmaal: Proceedings of the Conference on the 40th Anniversary of Somali Orthography, Djibouti, 17th–21st December 2012*, pp. 36–

48. Djibouti: Akadeemiye-Goboleedka Af-soomaaliga (The Intergovernmental Academy of Somali Language).

Dubois, J., M. Giacomo, L. Guespin, C. Marcellesi, J.-B. Marcellesi, and J.-P. Mevel (1973). *Dictionnaire de linguistique*. Paris: Larousse.

Idris Youssouf Elmi (2007). Project of a dictionary of about 100,000 entries. *Science et Environnement* (Special Issue on the Occasion of the 30th Anniversary).

Puglielli, A. (2015). Somali language studies past and future lexicography in the foreground. In *Afmaal: Proceedings of the Conference on the 40th Anniversary of Somali Orthography, Djibouti, 17th–21st December 2012*. Djibouti: Akadeemiye-Goboleedka Af-soomaaliga (The Intergovernmental Academy of Somali Language).

Rooxaan

Jaamac Muuse Jaamac

Hargeysa Cultural Centre
jama@redsea-online.org

This article was originally written in Somali and was translated by Martin Orwin.

Abstract

This very brief outline shows the potential of the Corpus of Somali Language which has been developed and is based at the Hargeysa Cultural Centre in looking at language use in literary and other texts. Some of the tools available have been applied to the story *Rooxaan* by Shire Jaamac Axmed and a brief overview is given here of issues relating to depositing written works into the repository and the sort of information that results from use of the tools available.

1 *Rooxaan*

The story *Rooxaan* 'Spirits' (Shire Jaamac Axmed, 1973b) is one of the written works chosen to be part of the project for the repository of Somali literature and its words. The work was written by Shire Jaamac Axmed and published by the Ministry of Culture and Higher Education in Mogadishu in 1973. Shire wrote a number of books and is remembered as the publisher of a journal which came out in the late 1960s in Somalia called *Iftiinka Aqoonta* 'The Light of Knowledge' (1966-7). He wrote two stories: *Rooxaan* 'Spirits' and *Halgankii Nolosha* 'The Struggle of Life' (Shire Jaamac Axmed, 1973a). He also played an important role, as a member of the different Somali language committees, in the choice of writing system which was to be adopted for the Somali language.

The Repository of Somali Literature and its Words is a research project based on the Corpus of Somali Language housed in the

Hargeysa Cultural Centre. It is a repository in which the words of Somali from the corpus are archived along with details of their morphology, etymology and categorization into parts of speech. Details are also stored of how each word is used in different contexts: poetry and prose, academic use, entertainment, official use and scientific research, fictional stories, essays, written and oral literature. It includes works already written and/or published and works which were originally in unwritten (oral) form and which have been written specifically for this project, e.g. the work of poets which has been transcribed.

The method used for entering *Rooxaan* was first to make a copy of the book published in Mogadishu and then to have it read by the optical character recognition application 'ABBYY Finereader 12' which captures the imaged letters. After that the spelling was corrected in all the places the software had made a mistake, comparing it with the original publication. The words which were changed were only those ones below which are spelling or typographical mistakes. The label [n:m] shows the place in the published version where something has been changed ('n' indicates the page number and 'm' indicates the line number).

[1:3] shire > Shire; [3:28] inuu uga jawaabo wiilkiisu weydiiyey > inuu uga jawaabo [su'aasha] wiilkiisu weydiiyey; [4:4] raca > raaca; [5:5] Saaleh > Saalax; [5:7] shiikh > Shiikh; [6:38] ayuu a aaminsanaa > ayuu u aaminsanaa; [7:36] Isagi > isagu; [9:1] Maandow > Maandhow; [9:26] haddi > haddii; [9: 28] naagod > naagood; [10:17] carrurta > carruurta; [10:31] shiikh > Shiikh; [14:16] Wuu joogaa? > Wuu joogaa.

Finally this present brief analysis does not concern the topic of the story; it is limited to the way the piece has been crafted and the use of words by the author. The importance is in the archiving of this piece of writing in which we see a high quality of both the craft of writing and the handling of the topic; it can be described as one of the finest pieces written in the Somali language.

Words which require comment but which have not been changed are given below.

1. [3:1] `Waalidyadiis` might correctly be `Waalidkiis` because the latter is a word mostly used for the plural.

2. [14:14] `marakan` > this is now generally spelled `markan`. `Marakan` seems to me to be colloquial or 'street' language.

3. The use of the spelling Muqdishow rather than Muqdisho is an interesting matter.

Interesting words which merit further consideration are given below.

1. [3:6] `yaleex jilicsan` > the word `yaleex` which is synonymous with `yix` is not in the corpus apart from the dictionary entry.

2. [3:24] `afjigi jirey` > the verb `afjigi` is now being used less, with the word `cabbudhi` being used instead. The most appropriate meaning is given in Cabdalla Cumar Mansuur and Puglielli (2012) 'afjig f.g1 (-gay, -gtay) Qof hadlaya, iyadoo loo diidayo inuu sheego sir ama wax aan habboonayn hadal ka joojin.'

3. [4:6] `ku jilnaa` > `jilnaa`, the word `jilan` which means 'living with someone' is used little these days.

4. [4:32] `illowse` > the author uses this word for `hase yeeshee` or `laakinse` but I hadn't come across this structure before. He has used it in a few places. See Figure 3 for the concordance of the word `illowse`.

5. [5:6] `idilu` > I would write `idili`. It doesn't seem to be a wrong spelling because analogous uses of `-u` are found (see [9:12] below).

6. [6:8] `baabuurka gaarigiisa` > it might be thought that these two words `gaari` and `baabuur` would now be used as synonyms whereas Shire Jaamac recognized the difference between the cab of a lorry and it's body.

7. [9:12] `lehu` > I would write `lehi` though it doesn't seem like a spelling mistake (cf. [5.6] `idilu` above).

The total number of words the author used comes to 3820 with 1345 of these words being distinct. The five most used words are `wuxuu` (116), `Guhaad` (104), `oo` (92), `ayuu` (91) and `ku` (8). Figure 1 shows the concordance for the word `wuxuu`.

Figure 2 shows the most common pairings of words from which the five most numerous in order are: 'Shiikh Muxsin', 'wuxuu ku', 'Shiikh Saalax', 'Guhaad wuxuu' and 'ka soo'.

Finally, Figure 3 shows the concordance of the word `illowse` and how the author used it where otherwise `haseyeeshee` or `laakinse` might be used.

Bibliography

Cabdalla Cumar Mansuur and A. Puglielli (2012). *Qaamuuska Af-Soomaaliga*. Rome: Roma TrE-Press.

Shire Jaamac Axmed (1973a). *Halgankii Nolosha*. Xamar: Wasaaradda Hiddaha iyo Tacliinta Sare.

Shire Jaamac Axmed (1973b). *Rooxaan*. Xamar: Wasaaradda Hiddaha iyo Tacliinta Sare.

Figure 1: Concordance for the word `wuxuu`

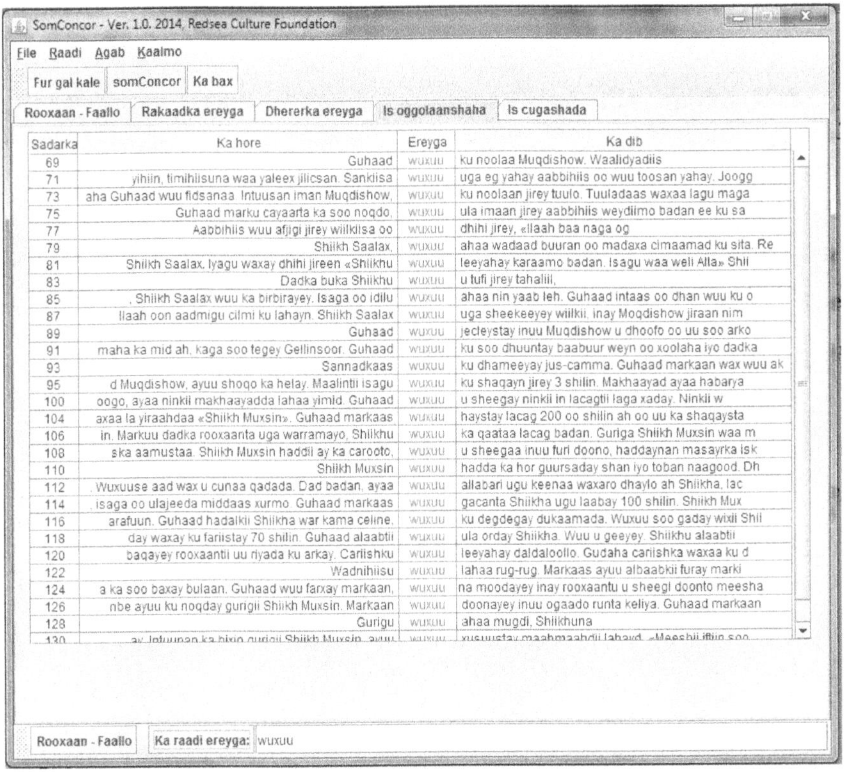

Sadarka	Ka hore	Ereyga	Ka dib
69	Guhaad	wuxuu	ku noolaa Muqdishow. Waalidyadiis
71	yihiin, timihiisuna waa yaleex jilicsan. Sankiisa	wuxuu	uga eg yahay aabbihiis oo wuu toosan yahay. Joogg
73	aha Guhaad wuu fidsanaa. Intuusan iman Muqdishow,	wuxuu	ku noolaan jirey tuulo. Tuuladaas waxaa lagu maga
75	Guhaad marku cayaarta ka soo noqdo,	wuxuu	ula imaan jirey aabbihiis weydiimo badan ee ku sa
77	Aabbihiis wuu afjigi jirey wiilkiisa oo	wuxuu	dhihi jirey, «Ilaah baa naga og
79	Shiikh Saalax,	wuxuu	ahaa wadaad buuran oo madaxa cimaamad ku sita. Re
81	Shiikh Saalax. Iyagu waxay dhihi jireen «Shiikhu	wuxuu	leeyahay karaamo badan. Isagu waa weli Alla» Shii
83	Dadka buka Shiikhu	wuxuu	u tufi jirey tahaliil,
85	. Shiikh Saalax wuu ka birbirayey. Isaga oo idilu	wuxuu	ahaa nin yaab leh. Guhaad intaas oo dhan wuu ku o
87	llaah oon aadmigu cilmi ku lahayn. Shiikh Saalax	wuxuu	uga sheekeeyey wiilkii, inay Moqdishow jiraan nim
89	Guhaad	wuxuu	jecleystay inuu Muqdishow u dhoofo oo uu soo arko
91	maha ka mid ah, kaga soo tegey Gellinsoor. Guhaad	wuxuu	ku soo dhuuntay baabuur weyn oo xoolaha iyo dadka
93	Sannadkaas	wuxuu	ku dhameeyay jus-camma. Guhaad markaan wax wuu ak
95	d Muqdishow, ayuu shoqo ka helay. Maalintii isagu	wuxuu	ku shaqayn jirey 3 shilin. Makhaayad ayaa habarya
100	oogo, ayaa ninkii makhaayadda lahaa yimid. Guhaad	wuxuu	u sheegay ninkii in lacagtii laga xaday. Ninkii w
104	axaa la yiraahdaa «Shiikh Muxsin». Guhaad markaas	wuxuu	haystay lacag 200 oo shilin ah oo uu ka shaqaysta
106	in. Markuu dadka rooxaanta uga warramayo, Shiikhu	wuxuu	ka qaataa lacag badan. Guriga Shiikh Muxsin waa m
108	ska aamustaa. Shiikh Muxsin haddii ay ka carooto,	wuxuu	u sheegaa inuu furi doono, haddaynan masayrka isk
110	Shiikh Muxsin	wuxuu	hadda ka hor guursaday shan iyo toban naagood. Dh
112	. Wuxuuse aad wax u cunaa qadada. Dad badan, ayaa	wuxuu	allabari ugu keenaa waxaro dhaylo ah Shiikha, lac
114	. isaga oo ulajeeda middaas xurmo. Guhaad markaas	wuxuu	gacanta Shiikha ugu laabay 100 shilin. Shiikh Mux
116	arafuun. Guhaad hadalkii Shiikha war kama celine.	wuxuu	ku degdegay dukaamada. Wuxuu soo gaday wixii Shil
118	day waxay ku fariistay 70 shilin. Guhaad alaabtii	wuxuu	ula orday Shiikha. Wuu u geeyey. Shiikhu alaabtii
120	baqayey rooxaantii uu riyada ku arkay. Cariishku	wuxuu	leeyahay daldaloollo. Gudaha cariishka waxaa ku d
122	Wadnihiisu	wuxuu	lahaa rug-rug. Markaas ayuu albaabkii furay marki
124	a ka soo baxay bulaan. Guhaad wuu farxay markaan,	wuxuu	na moodayey inay rooxaantu u sheegi doonto meesha
126	nbe ayuu ku noqday gurigii Shiikh Muxsin. Markaan	wuxuu	doonayey inuu ogaado runta keliya. Guhaad markaan
128	Gurigu	wuxuu	ahaa mugdi, Shiikhuna

Figure 2: The most common pairings of words

Heerka	Is cugashada lammaanaha	Kalgalka	Horraad	Danbeed
5.554588851777638	shiikh muxsin	29	69	34
3.0000000001	wuxuu ku	22	116	87
5.459431618737297	shiikh saalax	20	69	25
1.584962500821156	guhaad wuxuu	12	104	116
2.321928094987362	wuxuu u	12	116	74
3.700439718241092	ka soo	11	73	43
5.614709844215208	markii uu	11	23	37
4.523561956157013	wuxuu ahaa	10	116	14
3.0000000001	guhaad wuu	10	104	41
2.321928094987362	ayuu u	10	91	74
3.906890595708518	waxaa ka	9	30	73
4.906890595708519	ku arkay	9	87	13
1.584962500821156	ayuu guhaad	8	91	104
2.807354922157604	ku soo	7	87	43
4.0000000001	ku yiri	7	87	19
1.584962500821156	ayuu ku	7	91	87
2.807354922157604	waxay ku	7	40	87
2.807354922157604	waxay ka	6	40	73
1.0000000001	wuxuu ka	6	116	73
2.807354922157604	wuu ka	6	41	73
4.584962500821157	isaga oo	6	10	92
3.0000000001	ah oo	6	30	92
4.906890595708519	u sheegay	6	74	10
4.321928094987363	guhaad markaas	6	104	11
7.894817763407945	maxaa yeelay	5	10	8
2.584962500821156	saalax wuxuu	5	25	116
3.321928094987363	shiikhu wuxuu	5	16	116
4.643856189874724	weyn oo	5	8	92
2.584962500821156	waxay u	5	40	74

Ka saar midh kaliyaalaha | Tax dhammaan

Rooxaan - Faallo | Ka raadi ereyga: wuxuu

Figure 3: Concordance of the word `illowse`

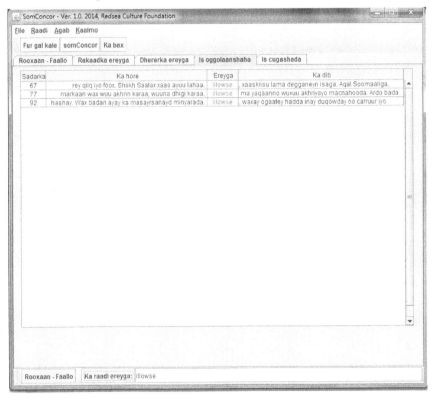

Language use of Somalis in Dollo Ado refugee camps: a sociolinguistic study of communication

Tirsit Yetbarek

Addis Ababa University (PhD candidate)
tysday@yahoo.com

Abstract

This article presents an overview of what has been written on the metre of the **geeraar**. The ideas presented in the literature differ in certain ways and

1 Introduction

This article is work in progress for a PhD dissertation in sociolinguistics that attempts to investigate the sociolinguistic situation of the Somali language focusing on dialect variation and its use in a particular Somali community in selected domains. The article provides a basic introduction to what triggered the research, how it fits into Somali language studies and how the whole project is to be accomplished. It gives more than just planned activities by incorporating a bird's eye view of accomplished tasks so far, even though the majority of the work is still in progress.

2 Background of the study

Language is a structured system of arbitrary symbols which is usually vocal. It is through this system that we interact and collaborate with others; in fact, a human group literally cannot cooperate in most circumstances without a common language. Generally, language has two functions: communicative and symbolic. While the communicative function facilitates the flow of information within a speech community, the symbolic function signifies the identity, preference and cultural aspects of a community. One important function of language is what Sapir has called a 'communicative function' (Sapir, 1921: p.7) and further says of language that it is 'the key to the heart of a people'.

Language is conceived as a purely human and non-instinctive method of communicating ideas, emotions and desires by means of a system of voluntarily produced symbols. This functional knowledge of a language assists in explaining the life-style and sociolinguistic situation of a community and implies that language does not operate independently of culture. Accordingly, incorporating the cultural aspect of language makes it clear that it is more than a means of communication. It helps us to see language through a pair of lenses: communicative function and symbolic function. In this regard Moulton (1974) defines language as a wonderful and rich vehicle of communication that allows the expression of ideas, wishes and commands, the conveyance of truths and lies, etc. He states that only human beings have that attribute of sending and receiving an unlimited number of messages. That is why the combination of the two functions helps to describe a community in depth, through its language use and its marks of identity contained in the language. That means cultural differences are inextricably bound up with language.

The interaction gets more interesting bearing in mind the fact that linguistic variation appears on several levels. Even within common-language groups, differences may be found at national, provincial and local levels, and these differences are manifested through dialectal differences. Dialect, sociolect and idiolect are among the mirroring realities which reflect different types of language use in various domains. This is the situation in which we find Somali society, which is assumed to be monolingual but has significant variation mainly on a dialect basis. Dialectal variation creates a situation where members may rank and choose among the dialects for a common communication channel in any given context. Accordingly, the factors initiating the inclination to use one or another variety in a certain domain are diverse but can be explained by a cost-benefit analysis by the individuals in that interaction. Therefore investigating language use in a particular society will significantly help to understand, define and inform socially significant policy directions regarding the language situation in any language community in general and in Somali-speaking communities in this particular case. It will also help to explain how significant dialectal variation could be a point of reference for in-group and out-group membership, which is usually the case in a general language variation domain but which might present a different outlook in the context of a presumed monolingual society.

It is with this base that the present author proposed a sociolinguistic study of Somali language, focusing on language use, dialect variation and their effects on language choice in different domains within a specific community.

The Somali language (`Af Soomaali`) is a member of the Cushitic branch of the Afro-Asiatic language family. It is thus related to Afar and Oromo and distantly related to Arabic. Since the arrival of Islam in the region, the Somali language has borrowed a large number of words from Arabic. It has also borrowed words from English, Italian and Indian languages, particularly during colonial times (Appleyard and Orwin, 2008, p.299; Fleming, 1976, p.43). In recent classification, Somali is grouped under the Eastern Omo-Tana branch of East Cushitic together with Rendille and Boni (Tosco, 2012: 265).[1]

Somali language experts have separated the dialects into two major groups: one is Af-Maxaad-Tiri and the other is Af-Maay (see Tosco, 2012: p.268). The two are considered dialects of the same language by some scholars even though the speakers of the two dialects have limited mutual intelligibility (Tosco, 2012; Appleyard and Orwin, 2008: p.299). There are also other significant scholars who strongly suggest considering Af-Maay as a separate and independent language on its own even though there is no consensus.

Scholars have classified the Somali dialects in different ways. According to Tosco (2012) the first scholar to classify the Somali dialects was the Italian Orientalist Enrico Cerulli, who, in 1919, classified Somali dialects based on clan differences: Isaaq, Daarood, Hawiye and Sab. Moreno (1955) divided the Somali dialects in the same

---

[1]According to Tosco (2012: p.265) Dhaasanac, Arbore and Elmolo belong to Western Omo-Tana and Baiso belongs to Central Omo-Tana.

way as Cerulli, but labelled Hawiye as Banaadir, and Sab as Digil which shows a combination of clan and geographic markers. Nevertheless, Andrzejewski (1971) challenged this clan-based classification and proposed a three-way distinction: Common, Coastal and Central Somali. Although clan names were excluded, there were no pure classifications since both Common and Coastal Somali belong to what Somalis traditionally call the Af-Maxaad-Tiri dialect. Later, Saeed (1982) replaced Andrzejewski's Coastal with Banaadir (see Tosco, 2012, pp.269–70). Saeed (1993: p.2) categorized the Somali dialects into three main groups: Northern (or Northern Central), Benaadir (Coastal) and Maay. In this classificatory scheme, Northern Somali forms the basis for the common Somali that is spoken in the Somali Regional State of Ethiopia, Djibouti, Northern and parts of Central Somalia and parts of Northern Kenya. Benaadir Somali is spoken on the southern coast of Somalia. On the other hand, Af-Maay is principally spoken in parts of the southern areas of Somalia and in the adjacent parts of Ethiopia and Kenya also.

Lamberti (1986: pp.26–30) also divides Somali dialects in a similar pattern but chose to divide them into five groups which are not dependent on lexical differences but mainly on phonological, syntactic and morphological traits. Accordingly, he has come up with the Northern Somali group, the Benadir group, the Ashraf dialects, the Maay dialects and the Digil groups. Acknowledging the need for further studies and supporting data, the present author believes that a combination of two specific perspectives might be followed: clan-based names suggested for the dialects in Somali language as presented by scholars such as Fleming (1964) and the combination of geographic and clan/sub-clan naming given to the dialects by scholars like Lamberti (1986). It is suggested that this might be the best way to understand dialectical variation in Somali in order to be able to understand the names of dialects which the researcher may come across during data collection in the actual research site.

Fleming (1964: p.36) gives the following, mostly clan-based, dialects for Somali language: Isaq (of Berbera), Benadir, Darod, Digil, Ašrâf, Jiddu, Jabarti, Mijurtein, Hawiya, Mediban (of Jigjiga). While Lamberti (1986) p.13-14 presented five dialect groups named as the

Northern dialects, the Benaadir dialects, the Ashraaf dialects, the May dialects and the Digil dialects comprising Af-Tunni, Af-Dabarre, Af-Garre and perhaps Af-Jiiddu. Hence, the combination of the two is a good foundation to understand the existence of multiple dialects of Somali language.

Regarding the written aspect of Somali language, in the middle of the twentieth century, when the need to write Somali increased considerably, various people began to develop writing systems. These were based on the Arabic alphabet or the Latin alphabet or were invented indigenous writing systems. Arabic script had been used for Somali to a certain extent prior to this, but not in any systematic or standardized way, and it was with a view to achieving a standardized orthography that various attempts were made to develop a writing system based on Arabic, which could then stand as a candidate for official acceptance. The attempt to establish a common orthography for the language reached a conclusion in 1972 when the military regime of Mohamed Siyaad Barre decreed that the Latin alphabet be used.

3 The clan system

The clan system can be both a stabilizing and destabilizing force. It's potential for destabilization lies primarily in the capacity of the clan system to serve as a conflict multiplier. The communal nature of the clan system means that an affront to an individual clan member can be interpreted as an affront to the entire clan, which draws the entire clan into what may initially be a minor dispute. On the other hand, an individual clan member is guaranteed economic, social and physical security for being born into the clan and has to defend the clan's interest. Social capital is conventionally regarded as a positive asset and in many instances it is. However, when it serves this function it can be a divisive element.

As is well known, Somali society is highly structured in the system of clans and sub-clans that bind and divide Somalis. It forms the basis for most of the core social institutions and norms of traditional Somali society, including personal identity, rights of access to local resources, customary law (*xeer*), blood payment (*diya / mag*) groups, and many other support systems (Gundel, 2006). The clan groupings of the Somali people are important social units, and clan membership plays a central part in Somali culture and politics. Clans are patrilineal and are divided into sub-clans, sometimes with many sub-divisions. The following are the six major Somali clans according to Lewis (1980): Daarood, Dir, Hawiye, Isaaq, Digil and Rahanweyn. Hundreds of clans, sub-clans, sub-sub clans etc. exist and allegiances are complex. Fundamentally, the strongest allegiance is to the lowest clan division (i.e. allegiance to the sub-clan is stronger than allegiance to the clan) but this is a somewhat simplified depiction and it is important to accept that clan practices are adaptable and dynamic, not static and timeless.

Clan life in Somali society is governed by the *xeer*, best understood as Somali customary law. The *xeer* is not formally codified but in reality often takes precedence over any laws created by the state. It is the set of rules, regulations and values that form the foundation of Somali society. *Xeer* can also represent agreements between sub-clans that govern their relations and lay out rules for interaction. At any particular time, two sub-clans may be allies or adversaries and these relationships are constantly shifting.

4   The underlying question for the study

As we have discussed above, the Somali community is considered to be a monolingual society with regards to its sociolinguistic composition. Nevertheless, we saw that some scholars argue that it is much more complicated, and that the various dialect situations are based on geography (Tosco, 2012; Andrzejewski, 1971; Saeed, 1982, 1993) or clan (Fleming, 1964). Dialect differences can be considered by examining the costs and benefits of adopting particular ways of speaking, which may differ for each individual speaker and in each individual situation. The aspiration to be included in a certain domain of communication instigates participants to devise a mechanism that grants them equal opportunity to express themselves and to be able to understand the dialogue to maximum potential. Therefore, existence of variation in language, dialect and even sociolect among participants of a communication endeavour is a driving factor in the choice of the language or dialect perceived as prestigious in any context. This choice is made with a view to a desired response, and preference is given to the variety that is believed to be assuring in terms of group belonging and identity.

This process of negotiation, apparent in the cost-benefit analysis that a communication participant makes with every encounter of variation is an interesting aspect of sociolinguistics. This could be the situation we find with the Somalis living in the Dollo Ado refugee camps. Here we might use these ideas to explain the pattern of dialect selection in the camp with regard to various domains of communication such as family, trade and education. Thus the research is concerned with language use in the camp with special focus on the dialectal variation of Somali vis-à-vis its social implications. Prestige and dominance among the dialects, language change patterns and related factors will also be investigated. The main research questions are given below.

1. What are the dialects currently used in the camp?

2. Which dialect is used in which domain?

3. How does the community member address the issue of varieties being used in the camp?

4. What dictates the choice of dialect by the community members?

5. What is the dominant dialect used in the refugee camp?

5   Methodology

Given the purposes of the research, there are two different orientations of sociolinguistic research which might be considered: qualitative (ethnography of communication, discourse analysis, etc.) and quantitative (language variation and change) approaches (Coupland and Jaworski, 1997: p.1; Trudgill, 2000: p.21; Chambers, 2003: p.ix). Given that the present research studies the sociolinguistic situation of a Somali-speaking community by focusing on dialectal variation, it is felt it demands an appropriate observational and interactional data collection method to determine a valid research output, thus a qualitative interactive research approach is felt to work best in this investigation. However there is also a demand for factual data regarding the pattern of dialect change as well as the types of dialect in the camp; this will be numerical in nature and is useful in determining the numbers of people speaking the different dialects in the community. The research therefore demands the combination of the two approaches, even though the basic and dominant character of the study is qualitative. This kind of inquiry is gaining prominence in scientific studies, since using a mixed research approach enables researchers to come up with an integrated data set when the need arises.

In order to collect data, the researcher will use in-depth interviews and observations combined together. General observations will be made in the camp to select a family that has diverse dialect composition with a significant generational depth of at least three generations from grandfather to grandchildren. It is assumed that this will assist the continuation of specific dialect use within the family and is a way of linking it to the different levels of communication groups: the elderly generation, the adult group and school-children. The participants for the in-depth individual interviews and observations will be selected based on age criteria: ten among schoolchildren, ten among adults and twenty to thirty among the age group of 40 and above. The final group will be given extra emphasis since it is assumed they retain the identity of their place of birth and origin which, it is suggested, is more strongly associated with clan and language variety than those of the other age groups who were either children when they arrived or were born and raised in the camp.

Based on their sociolinguistic significance, five domains will be investigated for this research. These are:

1. the official domain (communication between officials and community members);

2. educational domains;

3. media;

4. commerce and trade;

5. family.

Secondary data from documents on the sociolinguistics and use of language in the community will be used in the research. Audio recorder, notebook, photo camera and video recorder are the tools used for data collection. After data collection, software-based data translation will be implemented, which, during later analysis, will be categorized thematically for presentation.

This study is based in the Dollo Ado refugee camps, located in the Liban Zone of the Ethiopian Somali regional state, where more than 204,000 Somali refugees are living.[2] There are five camps within the Dollo Ado refugee camps complex. The two largest of the five camps are the Bokolmayo which was opened in 2009 and has a total of 41,665 refugees at the time of writing and the Melkadida camp which has 44,645 refugees and which serves as the central zone for administration for all the camps. Kobe, Heleweyn and Buramino are the other three camps with 39,214, 38,890 and 39,471 refugees respectively. The majority of the refugees are those who crossed the border from the Gedo region of Somalia, about 109,000 of the total population. The main reason for the selection of this research site is the fact that this place hosts three main Somali communities: those who came from Somalia (central and southern regions and Mogadishu), the Kenyan Somalis (from the north eastern district of Kenya) and Somalis from Ethiopia who work in the refugee camp and also live around the camps. This in turn signifies the presence of almost all Somali dialect-speaking communities and since most have stayed there for several years, due to the still unresolved peace situation, they have made their home there and have set in place all the structures of life in a Somali community.

---

[2]Statistics for the refugee camps can be found here: http://data.unhcr.org/horn-of-africa/documents.php?page=4&view=grid &Country%5B%5D=65 [last accessed 15 June 2017]. All numbers given in the text are at the time of writing.

It makes, then, a good context for the research questions and will hopefully provide some answers to them.

6 Significance of the study

This research will help to present a clear picture of the situation with respect to dialectal variation in the camp and the choice of specific dialects in certain domains. This will directly benefit the stakeholders, such as the government, NGOs and other actors who are interested in the conditions and situations in the refugee camp and in similar camps elsewhere. It will also hopefully help in formulating language-use policy at government level and assist communication and humanitarian aid delivery for NGOs working with Somali refugees in particular.

Linguistic research itself will also benefit from this study in that it will produce a sociolinguistic perspective of Somali-language use specifically in terms of dialect variation as it has developed in the last two decades or so for several reasons, in particular given the civil war in the central regions of Somalia.

Theoretical Framework Domain Analysis developed by Fishman (1965) provides observation tools for dialect variation based on the different domains of communication and will be used as a theoretical framework to discuss the choice and decisions community members make in using one or other dialects based on the situation.

In addition, ideas from the Poststructuralist framework will be used. This points out that society is asymmetrical in nature and languages and the speakers of language hold different levels of communicative power in different contexts within the social structure. Therefore, the notions of dominance and power in language use will also be used to elaborate on the situation in the camp. Romaine (1982) has demonstrated that people from such networks in their everyday encounters are largely dependent on the ways they use language with others with whom they interact. Furthermore, they have shown that social networks enable language users to manipulate each other and, as a result, linguistic change occurs. This new field of enquiry also has the potential to encompass research on all aspects of communication and language, from face-to-face interaction to historical and cultural change in language and its impact on language use.

7 Summary of findings so far

7.1 Varieties of dialects existing in the camp

Based on my observations and primary data obtained from the official sources, I have selected families with active interaction in the different camp environments along with the criterion of their being a family with parents who are from different dialect-speaking groups. I used a snowballing sampling system with the assistance of the Refugee Central Committee members in each camp. Therefore, in my stay at the refugee camp, I observed, recorded and conducted interviews with selected informants from whom I have a total of 28 recorded interviews. Based on this, I have managed to find out that the main naming for all the dialects is Af-Soomaali vs. Rahanweyn, which indirectly refers back to Af-Maxaad-Tiri and Af-Maay; these are the umbrella terms used for the dialect domains. However, it is also understood from further investigation that the Af-Soomaali which indicates the 'proper Somali dialect' connotation includes the Benaadiri Somali varieties. While the Rahanweyn varieties are the major varieties of Central Somalia along with those of Af-Ashraaf, Af-Gelede (Belede), Garre, Jiiddu and Dubo. All in all, the existence of various varieties is proved to be the case in the community. The dialect labelled 'Af-Soomaali', which indirectly refers to the Af-Maxaad-Tiri, is dominant in function since it is used in almost all domains. It is especially demanded and highly encouraged in the official or formal domains.

As mentioned above, there are five camps in Dollo Ado: Bokolmaayo, Buramino, Melkadida, Heleweyn and Kobe and I have visited all five camps to find informants based on the criteria and made interviews and observations in all of them. Based on this, I have found the Bokolmaayo camp, which was opened in 2009, to be the most dialectically varied since I have found Jiiddu, Dabarre, Garre, Gelede, Dubo and Ashraaf dialects in addition to the conventionally agreed

two major dialects in Somali language Af-Maay and Af-Maxaad-Tiri
dialects. Most of these dialects are already identified by previous
scholars except Dubo for which I have collected a word list as an
example presentation.

	Maxaad Tiri	Dubo
1.	caano	ceeno
2.	abuur	xashin
3.	geel	geel
4.	beer	jel
5.	wabi	wabaah
6.	istaag	roogso
7.	seexo	jiifo
8.	xagaa	hegaa
9.	caawo	cawada
10.	toddobaad	jilaaq
11.	qorrax	iriida
12.	maanta	beraah
13.	shalay	daraad
14.	shaah	rinsi
15.	kaalay	kooy
16.	madax	madaa
17.	timo	guud
18.	meeshan	inta
19.	xagga	hegaa
20.	farxad	faar faaraxeed
21.	murug	walbahaar

7.2   Dialect use in the domains

On the basis of the limited research already undertaken, I have found
that, the Af-Maxaad-Tiri dialect is the functionally dominant dialect
especially when considering the shared spaces, since it is the one used
in the official domain, the school domain and the market/trade domain. It seems to have this upper hand in the functional domain
because the writing of the language has been based on this variety
since 1972 when the central government of Somalia made it the of-

ficial national language. The school domain follows this direction and the curriculum is one used by the Ethiopian Somali government curriculum which made the Af-Maxaad-Tiri variety the medium for teaching and learning in Somali.

In the official domain there is some overlap between dialect and language difference. The main official language for communication between offices is English, while reports are sent to the federal government office in Amharic, since Amharic is the working language. This being the first layer of the language communication channel, when we look at the dialect aspect, again Af-Maxaaad-Tiri is the official dialect for official communication. When a refugee comes to the camp administration, for example during food distribution, the Af-Maay speaker is expected to use broken Af-Maxaad-Tiri to access services. This doesn't mean they are not allowed to use their own dialect, but the driving factor is that the assumed educated assistant workers are still from the Af-Maxaad-Tiri dialect domain and even those who are by birth Af-Maay speakers are recruited for official positions based on their capacity to speak Af-Maxaad-Tiri and additional languages.

7.2.1 The school domain

The school domain is one in which the choice of dialect and the issue of power and dialect is clearly apparent. There is a visible communication barrier in the camps when most students in a class are Af-Maay speakers but the curriculum uses Af-Maxaad-Tiri. The teachers are graduates who are recruited from among speakers of Af-Maxaad-Tiri but are teaching students the majority of whom are Af-Maay speakers. The school administration has identified the challenge students have with this dialect difference and has set in place a mechanism to address it by having two kinds of teachers. These are grouped under the name of 'national' and 'incentive' teachers. The 'national' teachers are those who are the lead instructors in all the subjects. They are instructors recruited and hired from among speakers of the Af-Maxaad-Tiri dialect group in line with the curriculum setup. The 'incentive teachers' on the other hand are those who are recruited from the refugee community to assist in addressing dialect-based difficulties in the teaching and learning environment and, if necessary, in translating from Af-Maxaad-Tiri to Af-Maay in order to assist the flow of information in teaching and learning. It seems that by dominance, power and related factors the Af-Maay speakers are expected more to understand Af-Maxaad-Tiri, which they have to work on more than the teachers.

7.2.2 The home and family domain

This is a very interesting domain in my observation. For one, it is where language and identity are clearly tied together and are presented by the individual. All the 'minor dialects' are used in this domain even though they may still be dominated by the main dialects. Therefore, this is the starting point to follow the dialect choice process. For example, a father who uses his own dialect, such as Garre, in the home uses Af-Maxaad-Tiri with friends in the neighbourhood, Af-Maay in the market domain, Af-Maxaad-Tiri when he goes to the school and uses English when he speaks to the camp administration. This chain of choice for dialect and language is based on the power, dominance and underlying status of the refugee versus the host community which has the official power.

7.2.3 The media domain

This domain is the one that is going to be contextually defined since there is no direct media targeting the group under study except the day to day notices and information exchange system which works more by word of mouth than through a structured line of communication. Hence this domain will be presented parallel to the official domain in due course instead of being treated as a separate domain.

7.3 Conclusion

The data gathering and analysis for this project is still in progress. Nevertheless there are initial indications of interesting outcomes to be discovered in terms of the language use in the community. The visible division between Af-Maxaad-Tiri and Af-Maay runs deep and there is much more to be said than what has been presented above.

References

Andrzejewski, B. W. (1971). The role of broadcasting in the adaptation of the Somali language to modern needs. In W. H. Whiteley (Ed.), *Language Use and Social Change: Problems of Multilingualism with Special Reference to Eastern Africa*, pp. 262–273. Oxford: Oxford University Press.

Appleyard, D. and M. Orwin (2008). The Horn of Africa: Ethiopia, Eritrea, Djibouti and Somalia. In A. Simpson (Ed.), *Language and National Identity in Africa*, pp. 267–290. Oxford: Oxford University Press.

Chambers, J. (2003). *Sociolinguistic Theory: Linguistic Variation and Its Social Significance*. Oxford: Wiley.

Coupland, N. and A. Jaworski (Eds.) (1997). *Sociolinguistics: A Reader and Coursebook*. Basingstoke: Palgrave Macmillan.

Fishman, J. A. (1965). Who speaks what language to whom and when. *La Linguistique 1*(2), 67–88.

Fleming, H. C. (1964). Baiso and Rendille: Somali outliers. *Rassegna di Studi Etiopici 20*, 35–96.

Fleming, H. C. (1976). Cushitic and Omotic. In M. Bender, J. Bowen, and C. Cooper (Eds.), *Language in Ethiopia*, pp. 34–53. Oxford University Press.

Gundel, J. (2006). *The Predicament of the 'Oday': The Role of Traditional Structures in Security, Rights, Law and Development in Somalia*. Nairobi: Danish Refugee Council and Novib-Oxfam.

Lamberti, M. (1986). *Map of Somali Dialects in the Somali Democratic Republic*. Hamburt: Helmut Buske Verlag.

Lewis, I. M. (1980). *A Modern History of Somalia*. London: Longman.

Moreno, M. M. (1955). *Il somalo della Somalia: Grammatica e testi del Benadir, Darod e Dighil*. Rome: Istituto Poligrafico dello Stato.

Moulton, W. (1974). The nature of language. In M. Bloomfield and E. Haugen (Eds.), *Language as a Human Problem*, pp. 58–73. New York: W.W. Norton and Company.

Romaine, S. (1982). *Socio-Historical Linguistics: Its Status and Methodology*. New York: Cambridge University Press.

Saeed, J. (1982). Central somali: A grammatical outline. *Afroasiatic Linguistics 8*(2).

Saeed, J. (1993). *Somali Reference Grammar*. Kensington, Maryland: Dunwoody Press.

Sapir, E. (1921). *Language: An Introduction to the Study of Speech*. New York: Harcourt, Brace and Company.

Tosco, M. (2012). The unity and diversity of somali dialectal variants. In N. O. Ogechi, J. A. N. Oduor, and P. Iribemwangi (Eds.), *The Harmonization and Standardization of Kenyan Languages: Orthography and Other Aspects*, pp. 263–280. Cape Town: The Center for Advanced Studies of African Society.

Trudgill, P. (2000). *Sociolinguistics: An Introduction to Language and Society*. London: Penguin.

Metre and 'extrametricality' in the *geeraar*

Martin Orwin

SOAS, University of London
mo1@soas.ac.uk

Abstract

This article presents an overview of the different ideas presented in the literature on the *geeraar* metre in Somali poetry. Following this a proposal is made which, it is suggested, provides a more accurate view of the behaviour of this metre and the way it displays the notion of 'extrametricality'. This latter issue was, albeit in different words, first introduced in Maxamed Xaashi Dhamac 'Gaarriye' (1976a). An analysis of a famous *geeraar* poem will show how the ideas work in practice.

1 Introduction

I shall begin by considering the proposals in the literature on the metrical pattern of the *geeraar*. Most of them differ in some details from one another, and I shall summarize these views and then present a metrical pattern which hopefully brings us to a more precise understanding of how this metre behaves. I shall also concentrate on one aspect of this which was presented in the first published account (Maxamed Xaashi Dhamac 'Gaarriye', 1976a). This is the proposal that certain grammatical particles are considered not to count with respect to the metre. This is the only such suggestion that has been made with regard to any metrical pattern in Somali poetry and requires bringing to the fore of research in the field along with an assessment of its validity. I suggest that, at least in the *geeraar* poems I have examined, this holds and is an example of extrametricality in Somali. By extrametricality what is meant is that parts of a line labelled as such play no role in determining the metricality of the line.

At the end I present a poem by Faarax Nuur which illustrates these points in more detail and shows how, in this poem, the metre, syntax, extrametricality and line grouping interact and are patterned.

Following Fabb (2015), I consider the line as the basis of any form of verbal art in any language which we might call 'poetry' in English. As a unit, this is determined in different ways in different languages. In Somali it is determined by metre, by which is meant the structured patterning of prosodic phonological entities which determines whether any given line is perceived as metrical or not. In Somali, the entities which are patterned are, informally, long- and short-vowel syllables and short-vowel syllables which end in a consonant.[1] Note that the notion of the line assumed here does not depend on writing, though it may subsequently be rendered in written form which does no disservice to poetry in Somali, even that made without recourse to writing in the original (see Orwin (2005) for more on this issue).

I shall not consider here the interaction between musical performance and metre and the line. This is an important feature for a full understanding of the performance of poetry when music plays a role, but it is not necessary to understand the abstract metrical structure of the line itself which is assumed solely to be a linguistic matter.

2   The metre of the *geeraar*

In this section, I shall consider the metre of the *geeraar* beginning with an overview of what has been written on the pattern so far and concluding with what I consider to be a matrix which characterizes the metre. This is not to say that this will be a definitive matrix since it is possible that there are some variations in the practice of certain poets or in certain regions which differs in some way to what is presented here.

Before continuing it is important to mention that, as reported in a number of works, the *geeraar* was traditionally recited on horseback in the past. Gamuute, for example, says the following on this: 'A distinct beat that resonates the rhythmic falling of the hooves of

---

[1]The presentation here is atheoretical and so I shall not consider these in more abstract terms such as morae.

a cantering horse, distinguishes Geeraar. In fact, a warrior on a charger, reciting Geeraar, is the image that comes to mind from my childhood.' (Farah Ahmed Ali 'Gamuute', in press: p.77).

2.1 J.W.C. Kirk

The first mention of the *geeraar* in the written literature on Somali is in Kirk (1905) in a chapter entitled 'Songs' (pp. 170-183). He writes of *geeraar, gabay* and *hees* that: 'a distinctly poetical style is noticeable' (p.170) and that 'All three seem to have a somewhat similar rhythm...' (p. 171). It is the mention of rhythm which is interesting here in that he seems to be picking up on what he perceives to be a rhythmic pattern shared by all forms, despite the observation that 'The length of the whole line may vary considerably.' (p.171). He doesn't present distinct metrical patterns and it cannot be determined from his writing whether the rhythm he is picking up on is in the language itself or in the performance mode which, at the time of his writing, can be assumed to have been with the *luuq*, the musical mode of recitation, or chanting mode. Given our present knowledge, we know that *geeraar* and *gabay* are quite distinct metrically and also that there are various forms of *hees*.

2.2 Maxamed Xaashi Dhamac 'Gaarriye'

The first published account of the metrical patterning of the *geeraar* is in Maxamed Xaashi Dhamac 'Gaarriye' (1976a). Although it has been referenced in work subsequent to it, not all the ideas presented have been take up by other researchers; this is therefore the first discussion of these ideas since that original article.[2] Before considering what Gaarriye wrote on the *geeraar* specifically, it must be mentioned that other metrical patterns had been discussed by him in articles published previously, and the ideas presented in those, although not directly referred to in his article on the *geeraar*, need to be kept in

---

[2]Gaarriye's article is republished, along with other of his work and poetry, in Cabdiraxmaan C. Faarax 'Barwaaqo' (2015). Cabdiraxmaan also developed software which checks metrical patterning, including the *geeraar* (see www.halgeri.com/laaxi.asp).

mind.[3] In particular the constraints on syllable-final consonants in the *jiifto* metre (and implied in related metres) expressed as constraints on consonant clusters and geminate consonants in Maxamed Xaashi Dhamac 'Gaarriye' (1976b) will be considered below.

The matrix presented in Maxamed Xaashi Dhamac 'Gaarriye' (1976a) is given in Figure 1. In this the number 2 represents a long-vowel syllable and 1 a short-vowel syllable. The vertically arranged sets of these units represent alternatives which he says may appear in those metrical positions. The central linear sequence '2112' indicates the invariable 'core' sequence of syllables: a long-vowel syllable followed by two short-vowel syllables followed by a long-vowel syllable.

Figure 1: Gaarriye's *geeraar* matrix

11		0
12	——	1
21	2112	
111	——	2

Two example lines which illustrate this are given in 1 taken from the poem by Faarax Nuur discussed in Section 3. The lines are given with Gaarriye's representation of the syllables in a manner which reflects the groupings in Figure 1.

(1)   a. Iska seexo idhaa: 11   2112 (1.5)

   b. Salaantaan badiyaa: 12   2112 (1.24)

Aside from the matrix, he also adds the following comment.

> Waxaan haddaba kaaga sii digayaa inay erayo xagga dambe ka raaca baydka geeraarka ah oo naxwahaan ku xidha baydadka ka dambeeya. Hase ahaatee miisaan ahaan kuwaasi uma baahna baydku. Waxa ka mid ah ereyadaas, (oo, ee, eey, baa, buu, baan, bay) iyo qaar kale oo badan.

> (Maxamed Xaashi Dhamac 'Gaarriye' (1976a: p.3))

---

[3]The metrical patterns are *jiifto, haantii qaboy, naa laago laago, maqalay warlay* and *gabay.*

Still I caution you that there are words at the end of the *geeraar* line which are grammatically linked to the following line. However, with respect to metre the line doesn't need them. Some of these words are (oo, ee, eey, baa, buu, baan, bay) and many others.[4]

What he is talking about is something that we might term extrametricality as mentioned above. Furthermore, we shall see below that, at least for the poems considered here (and all the poems I have looked through) his assertion regarding these words stands. The list he gives includes conjunctions (oo and ee), what I assume to be the feminine vocative ending (-eey) and the focus marker baa with and without subject pronouns.

2.3 Cabdillaahi Diiriye Guuleed 'Carraale'

The work of Cabdullaahi Diiriye Guuleed 'Carraale' on the *geeraar* can be found in a number of publications all of which are very similar and present his ideas on metre in Somali poetry in the same way. Here we shall take his most recent work, Cabdillahi Diiriye Guuleed (2016) as being representative. He states there are three types of *geeraar* line and one variant, what he terms *farcame*. As in all his work, he shows the metre by presenting the proportion of syllables to long vowels along with reference to the positions in which the long vowels can appear, though he doesn't present the latter with a matrical representation rather alludes to the syllable which has a long vowel (the 1st, 3rd etc.). So, of the lines he labels lix-saddexle 'with six-three', i.e. lines with six syllables of which three are long-vowel syllables, he gives the examples in 2 with long vowels underlined (p.92).

(2)   a. 6,3 = <u>Waa</u> bad-<u>baa</u>-do qab-<u>naa</u> (tusmada 1aad, 3aad, 6aad)

      b. 6,3 = <u>Saa</u>-xir-<u>kii</u> na-ga <u>guur</u>

      c. 6,3 = Sha-<u>luu</u> <u>taa</u>-gan a-<u>haa</u> (tusmada 2aad, 3aad, 6aad)

---

[4]All translations are by the present author.

d. 6,3 = Sa-<u>laan-tuun</u> ba-di-<u>yaa</u>

For his toddoba-labaale 'with seven-two' he has the forms in 3.

(3)   a. 7,2 = Rag-na <u>guur</u>-ka ma <u>daa</u>-yo (tusmada 3aad, 6aad)

    b. 7,2 = la-ba-<u>daad</u> wax ku <u>eeg</u>-to

He mentions a siddeed-kowle (8,1) as a base form (p.92) but gives no examples of this in the text or in the example poems.

The variant (*farcame*) line is a lix-labaale (6,2) which has as its base a toddoba-labaale (7,2) as in 4 (p.92).

(4)   a. 6,2 = Si-da <u>daad</u> u sab-<u>bee</u>
          7,2 = Si-da <u>daad</u> u sab-<u>bee</u>-ye

    b. 6,2 = Cu-li-<u>maa</u> a-jar <u>roon</u>
          7,2 = Cu-li-<u>maa</u> a-jar <u>roon</u>-e

With regard to the 'extrametrical' particles presented by Gaar-riye, Carraale doesn't mention these but he does seem to imply them in the example poems he gives in which he writes the conjunctions iyo and oo and the focus marker (with subject pronoun -aan) in parentheses in some examples. Although there is no comment on this, it seems to reflect the notion that these are not to be considered part of the metrical line. For example, the first line of the poem in Section 3 is written Rag sabaan ka sabaan (baan).

2.4   Cabdalla Cumar Mansuur

In 1977 Cabdalla Cumar Mansuur printed a revised and expanded copy of his dissertation which he had written in 1974-5 (Cabdalla Cumar Mansuur, 1977). One of the main parts which he added in his later work was detail of metrical patterning in light of the work of Gaarriye and Carraale which he had come to know.

He has a section on the *geeraar* in which he presents details which are interesting and include mention of the 'extrametrical' particles proposed by Gaarriye. He presents the *geeraar* as having a basic pattern of seven syllables but says that it can also have six or eight syllables subject to certain conditions.

1. Conditions on lines of six syllables.

    (a) Lines of six syllables end in the long vowel -aa. He mentions that for the most part such lines are at the end of a tix, a verse. As examples of such lines he includes some from Faarax Nuur's poem presented in Section 3.

    (b) The line can have six syllables when the line ends the verse but its ending is not -aa. These are very few.

2. Conditions on lines of eight syllables. A line may have eight syllables if:

    (a) the line ends in iyo, whether attached to the final word or not;

    (b) if at the end of the line there is one of the conjunctions oo or -na or the vocative ending -ow or -yow. He adds that if oo is present the line can be 7 or 8 syllables.

In addition to these conditions he states that: 'a line cannot begin with iyo or oo but that they can only occur at the end or in the middle of a line' (p.53). He gives the counter-example: 'Iyo guri xaajo xumaa' which he says is wrong because the line ends in -aa and needs to be 6 syllables and iyo at the beginning makes it 8.

With regard to the patterning of long- and short-vowel syllables he says there must be at least two long vowels in the line and that they must always be in the third and sixth positions. He also states (p.54) the line cannot have a long vowel in the fourth and fifth positions; this expresses the invariable core mentioned and implied by all other scholars.

2.5 John Johnson

Johnson has also presented work on the *geeraar* metre. The most recent configuration he gives is in Johnson (1996) where he presents what he terms the 'semic configuration' of the *geeraar* along with some other metres. The pattern of this configuration is as in Figure 2 of which he says 'a micron symbolizes a short vowel, and a macron symbolizes a long vowel; vertical lines separate semes and double vertical lines separate feet; the double spacing above the macron denotes closed-set disemes in which only long vowels may occur.' (Johnson, 1996: p.75).

Figure 2: *Geeraar* metre matrix in Johnson (1996)

$$\| \smile \mid \smile \mid \_ \| \smile \mid \smile \mid \_ \| (\smile)$$

His definition of a 'seme' is given as follows: 'The temporal duration of a short vowel, called a *mora* by *linguists*, occupies an amount of time called *seme* by students of prosody.' (p.75, emphasis in original). His notion of 'closed-set' here indicates that the diseme must be realized as a long-vowel syllable and may not be realized as two short-vowel syllables, as is the case with similarly looking metrical positions in other patterns such as the *jiifto*. Given this, the *geeraar* belongs to the set of metres which display what he calls a 'closed-set moro-syllabic' relationship. He gives two example lines which are given in 5.

(5) a. Nin habeenno casheeyay

b. Cadar aan hadh lahayn

Interestingly an earlier work, Johnson (1979), presents a greater number of variants for the *geeraar* line. In this work, he presents the metre in a foot-based manner positing eight possible feet (labelled A-H) for all metrical lines in Somali. Of these he says the following are used in the *geeraar*: C ($\smile\smile\_\smile$), E ($\smile\_\smile\smile$), F ($\smile\_\_$), G ($\smile\smile\smile\_$) and H ($\_\smile\_$). He gives the following sequences of these feet for the *geeraar*: C – F, C – E, F – G, G – C, F – C, C – E, H – C. These are given in our system of representation in Table 1. He also mentions that anacrusis and truncation may also occur (Johnson, 1979: p.49) in this metre, though this is not pursued apart from pointing this out following the sequences of feet (see Table 1). There is no mention of Gaarriye's suggestion regarding certain grammatical particles at the end of the line in any of Johnson's writings.

Table 1: *Geeraar* metre matrices posited by Johnson (1979)

C – F	◡◡_◡	◡_ _	
C – E	◡◡_◡	◡_◡◡	(with brachycatalexis)
F – G	◡_ _	◡◡◡_	(with anacrusis, "bad" line)
G – C	◡◡◡_	◡◡_◡	
F – C	◡_ _	◡◡_◡	
C – E	◡◡_◡	◡_◡◡	(with catalexis)
H – C	_◡_	◡◡_◡	

2.6 Francesco Antinucci and Axmed Faarax Cali 'Idaajaa'

Antinucci and Axmed Faarax Cali 'Idaajaa' (1986) give the metrical pattern as consisting of a nucleus of L B B L (where L stands for *lungo* 'long' and B for *breve* 'short') giving the following in our system: _◡◡_. The variants they posit are represented in Figure 3.

Figure 3: *Geeraar* matrix in Antinucci and Axmed Faarax Cali 'Idaajaa' (1986: p.35)

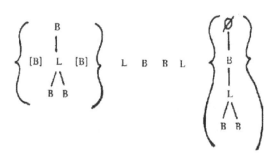

The middle part is fixed, as expected, and the line can be completed with syllables before and following the central core. These though are constrained by a total length of 8-10 vowel units. There is no mention of the nature of the syllables which follow the core and there seems to be the possibility of their allowing a single short-vowel syllable at the beginning of the line, something which is not allowed by any of the other proposals and doesn't seem to be a possibility in the metre. This will not be pursued further here.

2.7 Giorgio Banti and Francesco Giannattasio

Banti and Giannattasio (1996) present the most in-depth considera-tion of the *geeraar* metre to date and include analysis of performance with the *luuq*. With respect to the linguistic rather than the musical aspects of the metre, they present two sets of matrices, one based on the poems of Sayid Maxamed Cabdille Xasan and the other which takes into account variants from other poets they considered. Both sets are the same except for an additional optional long or short sylla-ble at the beginning of the line of poets other than Sayyid Maxamed Cabdille Xasan as shown in Table 2.

Table 2: *Geeraar* metre matrices given in Banti and Giannattasio

Matrices based on the *geeraar*s of Sayid M. C. Xasan
ᴗ̆ ᴗ̆ _ ᴗ ᴗ _
ᴗ̆ ᴗ̆ _ ᴗ ᴗ _ ᴗ̆
ᴗ̆ ᴗ̆ _ ᴗ ᴗ _ ᴗ ᴗ̆
Matrices based on *geeraar*s by other poets
(ᴗ̆) ᴗ̆ ᴗ̆ _ ᴗ ᴗ _
(ᴗ̆) ᴗ̆ ᴗ̆ _ ᴗ ᴗ _ ᴗ̆
(ᴗ̆) ᴗ̆ ᴗ̆ _ ᴗ ᴗ _ ᴗ ᴗ̆

Orwin and Maxamed Cabdullaahi Riiraash (1997) follow the pat-tern of Banti and Giannattasio in their presentation of the metrical pattern, they don't comment in detail on the pattern other than to say that, from the perspective of the 'Djibouti approach' to metrical study, it 'incorporates a section which is of the *chain* type of metre (this is the central core) along with aspects which are similar to the beginning of the *shubaal* line.' (Orwin and Maxamed Cabdullaahi Riiraash, 1997: p.97).

2.8   Faarax Axmed Cali 'Gamuute'

The final source of other work I shall consider is Farah Ahmed Ali 'Gamuute' (in press).[5] In this he approaches Somali metre from a foot-based perspective to describe and account for the structure of metrical lines. The *geeraar* is presented as being of two types: *geeraar* I and *geeraar* II. The first group is described as an anapaestic dimeter with the possibility of substitution in the first foot: 'The Anapest, Geeraar's dominant foot, can be replaced by the following feet: Bacchius, Amphimacer (acceptable through the syllabic caesura), and Molossus' (Farah Ahmed Ali 'Gamuute', in press: p.79). There is no substitution possible for the second foot. The second group accounts for variants of the line which have something following the final long-vowel syllable of the invariable part of the line. These are presented as trimetres with an initial foot comprising one of the following: anapaest, amphimacer, bacchius or molossus; the second foot an invariable dibrach and the final foot an invariable trochee. In a matrical representation of the type used here, this gives us the variants in Table 3.

Table 3: *Geeraar* patterns accounted for by Gamuute

geeraar I matrices	*geeraar* II matrices
∪∪_ ‖ ∪∪_	∪∪_ ‖ ∪∪ ‖ _∪
_∪_ ‖ ∪∪_	_∪_ ‖ ∪∪ ‖ _∪
∪__ ‖ ∪∪_	∪__ ‖ ∪∪ ‖ _∪
___ ‖ ∪∪_	___ ‖ ∪∪ ‖ _∪

What is interesting in this approach is the division between the two types of *geeraar* being expressed as presence of invariable feet at the end of each type of line. The lack of any substitution possibilities of these feet in conjunction with the fact that all the initial feet end in

---

[5]I am grateful to Gamuute for allowing me to present his work despite it not yet being published. He provides an interesting perspective on metre in Somali and it is hoped that his book, which is the product of extensive thought on the subject, will be published soon.

a long-vowel syllable expresses the invariable core of the *geeraar*. This might be interpreted such that anything that follows these patterns in a given line is considered not to be metrical. Gamuute may be leaving something unsaid that is apparent to him at some level, though of all the examples he gives, none have anything that goes beyond the line as he presents it. We might infer from this that, if, in any given poem or performance, something is present, it is regarded as extrametrical. This though is a mere suggestion here as there is nothing mentioned explicitly on this in Gamuute's section on the *geeraar*.

This concludes the overview of the *geeraar* metre as presented in the literature which gives specific patterns for it.

2.9   Syllable-final consonants in *geeraar*

The role of consonants in metre in Somali has been discussed with respect to the *jiifto* in Maxamed Xaashi Dhamac 'Gaarriye' (1976b), Orwin (2001) and Orwin and Mohamed Hashi Dhama 'Gaarriye' (2010). The constraint on syllable-final consonants has, however, not been considered in relation to the *geeraar* metre. Here we shall consider this issue given what is apparent in lines which the present author has considered and the constraint on the *jiifto* and related lines.

The constraint on syllable-final consonants for the *jiifto* metre can be expressed using an appropriate representation as in the matrix in Figure 4 (ignoring the optional short-vowel syllable at the beginning of the line which need not concern us here).

In this matrix there may be a consonant at the end of the first of the two short-vowel syllables in MP1 (metrical position 1) when that position is realized with two such syllables, hence the representation of this position as ᰨ. However, there cannot be a syllable-final consonant at the end of the first of the two short-vowel syllables in MP2, MP4 and MP5 when these are realized with two short-vowel syllables. A corollary of this relates to geminates and what have been termed virtual geminates (the consonants *t, k, f, s, sh, j, w* and some instances of *y*) which can only be present in positions in which a

Figure 4: Basic *jiifto* matrix

MP1	MP2	MP3	MP4	MP5
⏕	ᴗ̲	ᴗ	ᴗ̲	ᴗ̲

syllable-final consonant may occur.[6]

Given what we know of the *geeraar*, we can see that there are no metrical positions of the type in which, in the *jiifto* metre, the constraint can be said to hold or not to hold; that is to say there are no positions of type ⏕ or type ᴗ̲ .

As an intial hypothesis based on scanning a large number of lines we see that syllable-final consonants are allowed at the end of any syllable (and hence geminates and virtual geminates can be present in any position). Examples of lines are evident in the poem presented in Section 3.

2.10   Summary

Having considered what has been presented in the literature on the metre of the *geeraar* we can see that there are certain things which all the proposals share. They all include the invariable pattern _ᴗᴗ_ which we shall label here the *core* of the line and they all include extra syllables before and after this.

Table 4 gives the line-initial variants (that is the sequences of syllables that can precede the core) from all the works mentioned above that provide specific patterns. The sequences which are present in more than one work are labelled A-F and those found only in Banti and Giannattasio (1996) are labelled BG1-BG7. Table 5 shows the patterns accounted for in the works considered. Although he doesn't give a matrix or other abstract patterning as such, Carraale is included in this table on the basis of the analysed lines he gives

---

[6]All geminate consonants in Somali are heterosyllablic being formed of the coda consonant of one syllable followed by the onset consonant of the next, that is they are syllabified as CVC.CV(C) (where the vowels may be long or short) and so are also restricted given this constraint.

118

but not including all the possibilities seen in the examples he gives which he doesn't analyse or comment on.

Table 4: Line-initial variants with labels

Label	Pattern
A	∪∪
B	∪_
C	_∪
D	∪∪∪
E	_ _
BG1	_ _ _
BG2	∪_ _
BG3	_∪_
BG4	_ _∪
BG5	∪∪_
BG6	_∪∪
BG7	∪_∪

We see from this that the all works following the initial proposal of Gaarriye include the variants he presents at the beginning of the line apart from Gamuute and Carraale who don't account for D (∪∪∪).[7] Only Gamuute and Banti and Giannattasio allow for two long-vowel syllables (E) at the beginning. Banti and Giannattasio also have a large number of possibilities at the beginning of the line with all the logical possibilities of three syllables for poets other than Sayid M. C. Xasan, but they do comment on this and we shall return to it below.

Turning to line-final variants, these are given in Table 6 with labels. The possibilities presented by each author are given in Table 7. Gaarriye's matrix doesn't include patterns J and K (∪∪ and ∪_ respectively), but when we take his patterning in conjunction with the comments on the 'words at the end of the *geeraar* line which are grammatically linked to the following line' (see Section 2.2), both of

---

[7]There is one example line from Timocadde among Carraale's lines which displays ∪∪∪: **Samada kii u ekaayee** (p.95).

Table 5: Line-initial variants accounted for

Author(s)	Patterns accounted for
Gaarriye	A, B, C, D
Carraale	A, B, C
Johnson	A, B, C, D
Antinucci & 'Idaajaa'	A, B, C, D
Banti & Giannattasio	A, B, C, D, E, BG1–7
Gamuute	A, B, C, E

Table 6: Line-final variants

Label	Pattern
G	nothing
H	⌣
I	—
J	⌣⌣
K	⌣—

these are implied and are therefore added in parentheses.[8] Carraale accounts for G and H in his analysis. However, he also has examples which display the other possibilities (some in parentheses and some not) and, as mentioned in section 2.3 this may be taken as implying these parts of the line as extrametrical. Taking Johnson (1979) and Johnson (1996) together, we see he has all possibilities apart from K, as do Antinucci and 'Idaajaa'. Gamuute has the most restricted set of possibilities with just G and H (this is discussed further below). Only Banti and Giannattasio include all the possibilities for line-final variants in their matrices.

---

[8]We might consider K also to be implied if a focus marker is present at the end of a line following a short vowel (accounted for in his matrix).

Table 7: Line-final variants accounted for

Author(s) account for	Patterns author(s)
Gaarriye	G, H, I, (J, K)
Carraale	G, H
Johnson	G, H, I, J
Antinucci & 'Idaajaa'	G, H, I, J
Banti & Giannattasio	G, H, I, J, K
Gamuute	G, H

2.11   A consolidated proposal for the *geeraar* metre

Taking into account what others have proposed for this metre, along with having read many lines, leads me to posit a matrix for the *geeraar* which is given in Figure 5 along with a condition on what can follow the vertical line in the matrix. Curly brackets indicate that one or the other of the two options must be present; parentheses indicate that what is between them may or may not be present.

Figure 5: Matrix suggested here for the metre of the *geeraar*

$$\left\{ \begin{matrix} \smile\smile\smile \\ \sigma\sigma \end{matrix} \right\} -\smile\smile- \; (\smile) \; | \; \left(\begin{matrix} - \\ \smile \end{matrix} \right)$$

Condition: Any syllable following the vertical line must be or be part of a conjunction, a focus marker (with or without a subject verbal pronoun) or a vocative suffix.

We see in this the invariable core of the line which is preceded by the possibilities A, B, C, D and E of Table 4. Following the core, a single short-vowel syllable may be present ($\smile$) and after this is a vertical line followed by the possibility of either a long-vowel syllable or a short-vowel syllable. The vertical line here indicates the end what is considered to be the metrical line and what follows it is assumed to be extrametrical because of the condition. It is not the phonological nature of what follows the vertical line, but the syntactic role it plays that determines whether it is perceived as correct or not and so this perception is, strictly speaking, not metrical perception based on phonology hence the characterization of these possible syllables as extrametrical.

To illustrate this let us look at the examples in 6 in which each of the line-final possibilities is present.[9]

(6) a. Gugucdeeda arooryiyo

b. Isku gaagixinteeda

c. Away gooha wanaajaay

d. Gurxankii Habilaad

e. Hadduu saakimi waayona

f. Gabadh suurad wanaagsan baan

6d has no line-final syllables beyond the 'core' and has the metrical pattern ∪∪_∪∪_. We might consider this to be the basic line of the *geeraar* and it fits Gamuute's description of this line as essentially an anapaestic dimetre. Line 6b shows a line-final short-vowel syllable, thus the line scans as follows: ∪∪_∪∪_∪. We see that the final syllable is not a separate word or particle, but is the final part of the word **gaagixinteeda**, thus the optional final short-vowel syllable before the vertical line in the matrix is present. Line 6a has two short vowel syllables at the end, both of which comprise the single conjunction **iyo**. The 'i-' of which is the final optional short-vowel syllable before the vertical line and the '-yo' of which is in the short-vowel syllable position following the vertical line. The condition is met given that this final syllable is part of a conjunction. Another explanation for this is to say that the whole conjunction is extrametrical and that we allow for the possibility of two short-vowel syllables after the vertical line (which must still meet the condition). This will

---

[9]Examples lines 6a–6d are the first four lines of a *geeraar* by Raage Ugaas Warfaa (Axmednuur Maxamed 'Ustaad', 2015: p.107) and example lines 6e and 6f are from the *geeraar* by Faarax Nuur discussed in Section 3.

be left to future research.[10] Line 6c ends in a long vowel syllable but, in this case, it is a vocative ending and so meets the condition on the long-vowel syllable position following the vertical line.[11] Finally example line 6e is interesting in that it ends with two short vowel syllables but, although the word is written as one, they both belong to different constituents. The word **waayo** is the verb and its final vowel fills the short-vowel syllable position before the vertical line and **-na** is a phrase conjunction clitic and thus meets the condition on syllables following the vertical line.

Having presented examples that confirm the matrix assumed, we must also address the few examples given in Banti and Giannattasio (1996: p.100-1) which do not fit this matrix. Five lines in particular are interesting and are given in 7.[12]

(7)   a.   Caanihii gaasir noqdeen

       b.   Cambartii geela dhalaysiyo

       c.   Waa walaala aad ah

       d.   Saciira iyo naciima

They point out that the first three are from early poets: 7a and 7c from the nineteenth century, and 7b from the early twentieth century. If we consider 7a and 7b carefully we see one possible explanation is an extra short-vowel syllable in the first part of the line shown in

---

[10]Yet another possibility is that the **iyo** is pronounced as part of the previous word and being realized as **-yo** which is common in poetry. This will be left to future research also and is not considered to be an issue crucial to the main point being made here.

[11]It might be argued by some that given the fact that this ending is an open syllable diphthong it can count as short as well as long and so need not be stipulated as a separate possibility, but can be accounted for simply by being counted as a short vowel syllable and occupying the short-vowel syllable position before the vertical line. I would argue, for reasons I shan't go into here, that the vocative might be considered to be long in the majority of cases in other metrical patterns and assume this to be the case here. Also, considering it to be extrametrical fits with Gaarriye's original presentation as well as Cabdalla Cumar Mansuur's observation on the vocative mentioned Section 2.4 above.

[12]The poets and translations they give are: 7a Raage Ugaas Warfaa 'Milk that got scarce', 7b Salaan Carrabay 'Camels bearing young and', 7c Gidhish 'They are true brothers' and 7d Timocadde 'Hell and paradise'.

parentheses in these scansions: $\_(\smile)\_$ (Caanihii) and $\smile(\smile)\_$ (Cambartii) respectively. This may be said to be something similar to the extra short-vowel syllable which can be present in the first part of lines of the *jiifto* and related metrical patterns and so it might be added to the matrix in Figure 5. This may also be the explanation for the sequence of three short-vowel syllables at the beginning of the line, that is to say, one of them is an 'extra' short-vowel syllable and the other two are the two syllables (which can be long or short) at the beginning of the line in the matrix in Figure 5. Investigation on this point will be left to future work.

Gidhish (7c), they point out was from a different region to the other poets (Mudug and Galguduud) and this is the one which seems to have no other explanation than to be a variation, whether specific to the region at the time or to the poet. It's the most striking line because the difference lies in the core rather than at a periphery. I have no explanation for this and leave it to future consideration.

Turning finally to 7d it is not unlikely that, in performance this might be rendered 'Saciiraayo naciima' where the -a of 'Saciira' and the i- if 'iyo' become a long diphthong as this conjuction is often assimilated in some way with the previous word in poetry. On the other hand it may be, as they point out, 'a personal variant of Timocadde who, like many other major Somali poets, could freely introduce innovations into the received genres.' (Banti and Giannattasio, 1996: p.101).

3   A sample *geeraar* poem

In this section I shall consider a particular *geeraar* poem in detail, namely the famous 'Rag Sabaan ka Sabaan baan' by Faarax Nuur which has also been used as an example in some of the works discussed above. I shall look in particular at how the line-final particles are used and offer some observations. The full text of the poem is given below. The text has been divided into verse paragraphs which are labelled VP1-9 and every fifth line is numbered for convenience. The text and translation are taken from Rashiid Sheekh Cabdillaahi Xaaji Axmed and Ismaaciil Aw Aadan (2009: pp. 74-5). It has not been edited and so some of the spelling is not as would be expected. This is due to the spelling reflecting not only general pronunciation but the way certain parts are pronounced given that this is a *geeraar* poem. For example line 2 is written Salaantow badiyaa when if this were written in a more standard way it would be Salaanta u badiyaa. We can see that this is because of the metrical patterning. In the standard way of writing there are two short vowels where a long-vowel syllable is required, however, the ending of the definite article suffix -a and the following preverbal prepositional particle u may be pronounced in such a way that they sound like a dipthong and as such can be pronounced and count as a long vowel with respect to the metre.

Rag Sabaan ka Sabaan baan

VP1	Rag sabaan ka sabaan baan			Gabadh suurad wanaagsan baan	
	Salaantow badiyaa			Surrad'owga dhisaa	
VP2	Hadduu saakimi waayona		VP7	Hadduu saakimi waayona	
	Sariir baan u goglaayoon			Xoolo gooni u soofiyo	20
	Iska seexo idhaa	5		Sadadaan ku ladhaa	
VP3	Hadduu saakimi waayona		VP8	Hadduu saakimi waayona	
	Caanahii hasha Suub baan			Seeddoow Mood iyo Mood iyo	
	Saddex jeer u lisaayoo			Salaantaan badiyaa	
	Ku sarriigo idhaa		VP9	Hadduu saakimi waayona	25
VP4	Hadduu saakimi waayona	10		Salaaddaan lallabaayoo	
	Summalkii rugta joogiyo			Maydal seedo madow iyo	
	Sogobkaan u qalaa			Safkii aan ka dhashiyo	
VP5	Hadduu saakimi waayona			Salligaan cuskadaayoo	
	Sarreenkii Cadameed baan			Sulub eebo ku joogtaan	30
	Sixinkowgu badshaa	15		Sarartaa ku dhuftaayoo	
VP6	Hadduu saakimi waayona			Sanbabkaan ka baxshaayoo	
				Markaasuu sallimaa	

(Faarax Nuur)

Time and Time Again

Time and again to men
I give many greetings
If he fails to calm down
I set out a sleeping mat
for him
And say 'Just sleep'   5
And if he fails to calm
down
I milk Suub, the camel
For him three times
And say 'Drink from it'
And if he fails to calm
down   10
The ram that is at the
settlement
And the castrated billy
goat I slaughter for
him
And if he fails to calm
down
The wheat from Aden
I will mix with ghee for
him   15
And if he fails to calm
down
A girl of fine appearance
And mats for the bridal
hut I give to him
And if he fails to calm
down

I drive livestock to graze
just for him   20
And add them to the
share
And if he fails to calm
down
Oh brother-in-law 'Pass
peacefully' and 'Wel-
come'
I pile these greetings on
him
And if he fails to calm
down   25
At the time of the
prayers I announce
the *reer* is leaving
The grey horse with
black tendons
And the line I am born
of
And supporting myself
on the *salli*
With a spearhead of
iron   30
I strike his sides
And make his lungs
come out
And then he settles the
account

(Translated by Martin Orwin.[13])

[13] See (Rashiid Sheekh Cabdillaahi Xaaji Axmed and Ismaaciil Aw Aadan, 2009: pp. 194-5)

126

3.1 Line final particles

In this poem we find confirmation of both the matrix and the condition given in Figure 5.

The focus marker **baa** is found at the end of lines lines 1, 7, 14, 17 and 30, in each case with the 1st p.sg. subject verbal pronoun -aan giving **baan**. Note in line 30 `Sulub eebo ku joogtaan`, the **baan** assimilates with the verb form; the three parts of `joogtaan` are given in 8.

(8) `joogto baa        aan`
     verb   focus marker 1 sg subject verbal pronoun

We see the conjunction oo in lines 4, 8, 26, 29, 31 and 32. In line 4 `Sariir baan u goglaayoon`, the -oon is formed of oo and -aan as shown in 9.

(9) `goglaa oo        aan`
     verb   conjunction 1 sg subject verbal pronoun

The fact that it is written as part of the same word as the verb with the glide 'y' reflects the way such forms are pronounced when poetry is recited.

We also find the short-vowel conjunction -na at the end line 3 (and in the repeated instances of this line: 6, 10, 13, 16, 19, 22 and 25). The bisyllabic noun phrase conjunction **iyo** is also present in lines 11, 20, 23, 27 and 28.

All the instances of the extrametrical syllables here are either conjunctions or focus markers. Given the syntactic nature of these particles, it follows that extrametrical syllables are always found at the end of a line which is not at the end of a verse paragraph, that is where there is the expectation that that section of the poem will continue, where a subsequent line is necessary. It also follows from this that no line at the end of a verse paragraph or at the end of a poem can have such an extra-metrical syllable. This observation reflects Cabdalla Cumar Mansuur's comment on six-syllable lines ending in -aa (see Section 2.4) and also the comment in Banti and Giannattasio:

The distribution of types (20i–iii) in the **geeraars** composed by the Sayid is partly restricted, in so far as 6-syllable lines usually occur at the end of a stanza. Instead, 7- and 8-syllable lines alternate freely in other positions. It would appear that the Sayid established this typology for his **geeraars** by discarding some kinds of lines that were possible for the poets that preceded him.

(Banti and Giannattasio (1996: p. 100))

The matter of vocative endings is a little different, though it may be argued that a nominal ending in a vocative leads to an expectation of something being said to or of the nominal to which the vocative is added.

3.2 Practical stylistic analysis

It is one thing to demonstrate how the words used in any particular line are analysed as being metrical or not, but poets make use of the metrical and syntactic possibilities in structuring their poems and we see this clearly in the poem by Faarax Nuur.

We have seen that the lines can be grouped into verse paragraphs, as indicated in the text with VP1–9.[14] Each of the verse paragraphs, aside from the first one, begins with the repeated line: **Hadduu saakimi waayona**, which, as mentioned above, ends in the conjunction **-na**. Grammatically speaking this links the main clause in which it is found to the previous main clause. So the **-na** in line 3 links the main clause comprising lines 3–5 with the main clause comprising lines 1–2. When we look further at the lines we see that all except those that conclude a verse paragraph have at the end either a conjunction, a conjunction coalesced with subject verbal pronoun

---

[14]I choose to call these 'verse paragraphs' rather than stanzas since that term, for readers more familiar with European forms of poetry, can imply that the line groupings are of equal length which is not the case here. Having said that however, 6 out of the nine verse paragraphs are three lines in length. Where there is consistency in length of verse paragraph, this may be referred to in Somali: a poem with consistent verse paragraphs of three lines, for example, may be referred to as *saddexley* 'one of three', such as many of the *gabay* poems of Sayyid Maxamed Cabdille Xasan.

(as in **goglaayoon**), or a focus marker (in all cases with the 1. sg. subject verbal pronoun). All the lines that conclude the verse paragraphs end in main verbs with the long-vowel present tense ending -aa in the final part of the core metrical pattern ($\smile\cup\cup\smile$). We see this parallelism across all the verse paragraphs apart from the final one VP9.

Looking just at verse paragraphs 1–8, we see they all have the same basic syntactic structure with one or more main verbs in the 1st. p. sg. (joined by the conjunction **oo** where there is more than one main verb) and a focus marker. These are reproduced again in 10 with the main verbs, the conjunctions joining the main verbs and the focus markers all indicated. Some of the focus markers are not separate words, but are coalesced with the noun they are focussing (l. 12: **sogobkaan**, l. 21: **sadadaan**, l. 24: **salaantaan**).

(10)   VP1 Rag sabaan ka sabaan [baan]$_{focus}$
            Salaantow badiyaa

VP2 Hadduu saakimi waayona
      Sariir [baan]$_{focus}$ u [goglaa]$_{main\,v.}$y[oo]$_{conj.}$n
      Iska seexo [idhaa]$_{main\,v.}$

VP3 Hadduu saakimi waayona
      Caanahii hasha Suub [baan]$_{focus}$
      Saddex jeer u [lisaa]$_{main\,v.}$y[oo]$_{conj.}$
      Ku sarriigo [idhaa]$_{main\,v.}$

VP4 Hadduu saakimi waayona
      Summalkii rugta joogiyo
      Sogobk[-aan]$_{focus}$ u [qalaa]$_{main\,v.}$

VP5 Hadduu saakimi waayona
      Sarreenkii Cadameed [baan]$_{focus}$
      Sixinkowgu [badshaa]$_{main\,v.}$

VP6 Hadduu saakimi waayona
      Gabadh suurad wanaagsan [baan]$_{focus}$
      Surrad'owga [dhisaa]$_{main\,v.}$

VP7 Hadduu saakimi waayona
      Xoolo gooni u soofiyo

Sadad[aan]$_{focus}$ ku [ladhaa]$_{main\,v.}$

VP8   Haddu saakimi waayona
       Seeddoow Mood iyo Mood iyo
       Salaant[aan]$_{focus}$ [badiyaa]$_{main\,v.}$

Turning to VP9 we see that the syntactic structure is similar to
the previous verse paragraphs, but there is a subtle difference. The
verse paragraph is repeated in 11 with the same grammatical entities
indicated as in 10.

(11)   VP9   Haddu saakimi waayona
             Salaadd[aan]$_{focus}$ [lallabaa]$_{main\,v.}$y[oo]$_{conj.}$
             Maydal seedo madow iyo
             Safkii aan ka dhashiyo
             Sallig[aan]$_{focus}$ [cuskadaa]$_{main\,v.}$y[oo]$_{conj.}$
             Sulub eebo ku joogt[aan]$_{focus}$
             Sarartaa ku [dhuftaa]$_{main\,v.}$y[oo]$_{conj.}$
             Sanbabk[aan]$_{focus}$ ka [baxshaa]$_{main\,v.}$y[oo]$_{conj.}$
             Markaas[uu]$_{focus}$ [sallimaa]$_{main\,v.}$

Two things stand out from this final verse paragraph. Firstly,
there is a greater number of main verb clauses within the verse paragraph introduced by the repeated line Haddu saakimi waayona.
This, in my opinion, reflects the line's greater sense of urgency and
the change in tone. The verse paragraphs preceding give a sense of
patience in that each one presents a positive aspect of hospitality to
the person who 'fails to calm down' each of these being presented following the repeated introductory line. No matter how often the other
person irritates, the poet will offer excellent hospitality.[15] When the
final verse paragraph begins with the same repeated line, the expectation is that more will follow, the poet will continue to be hospitable,
however, this is not the case. Here the patience has run dry and we
have a series references and statements to the poet's resolve in retali-
ating against his opponent finishing with the gruesome lines Sarartaa
ku dhuftaayoo / Sanbabkaan ka baxshaayoo. The final line then

---

[15]I leave aside here discussion of voice and subjectivity in the poem. As oral
literature, the poet is in a real sense the voice in the poem when it was first
recited, but there is more to say on this subject with respect to Somali poetry.

turns things around dramatically. Prior to this line, the subject has always been first person, but in this line suddenly the subject is third person, the poet's adversary. This abrupt change given what has become a strong expectation of a first person subject reinforces the fact that the adversary, who was not satisfied with any of the hospitality offered, finally reaps the rewards of his intransigence.

The syntactic structure can be seen to interact with the metrical structure and the wider structuring of lines into verse paragraphs. Part of this structuring of the lines is evident in the use of the conjunctions and focus markers which are regarded as extrametrical. Use of these extrametrical syntactic particles and the concomitant lack of them in the final lines of verse paragraphs contributes to the flow of language in this poem.

4   Conclusion

In this paper a proposal for the metrical pattern of the *geeraar* has been presented which acknowledges previous work. There is more work to be done to fully understand the beginning of the line but, as it stands, the matrix in Figure 5 accounts for the vast majority of lines I have come across. The discussion on some lines given by Banti and Giannattasio shows us where further work is needed and also points to the possibility of regional and individual variation in how the metre is used. The other major point made in this paper was to show the way extrametricality plays a role in the *geeraar*. This dicussion is based on the original insight presented in Maxamed Xaashi Dhamac 'Gaarriye' (1976a). Other scholars seem to hint in some way or another at this characteristic but until now it has not been considered in more detail or presented as a formal feature of metrical patterning. Examples have been given of how this works in practice. It seems, as far as we know at present, that this feature is restricted to the *geeraar*. Why this should be, and indeed whether that is really the case, will be left to future research.

References

Antinucci, F. and Axmed Faarax Cali 'Idaajaa' (Eds.) (1986). *Poesia orale somala: storia di una nazione*, Volume 7 of *Studi somali*. Rome: Ministero degli affari esteri-dipartimento per la cooperazione allo sviluppo. Comitato tecnico linguistico per l'università nazionale somala.

Axmednuur Maxamed 'Ustaad' (2015). *Tix & Tiraab: Diiwaanka Gabayadii Raage Ugaas Warfaa iyo Taariikhdiisii.* Seattle.

Banti, G. and F. Giannattasio (1996). Music and metre in somali poetry. In R. Hayward and I. Lewis (Eds.), *Voice and Power: The Culture of Language in North-East Africa. Essays in Honour of B.W. Andrzejewski*, Number 3 in African Languages and Cultures Supplement, pp. 83–127. School of Oriental and African Studies.

Cabdalla Cumar Mansuur (1977). Astaamaha guud ee maansada soomaaliyeed.

Cabdillahi Diiriye Guuleed (2016). *Gibil Xidh: Miisaanka Maansada Soomaaliyeed.* Hargeisa: Sagaljet.

Cabdiraxmaan C. Faarax 'Barwaaqo' (2015). *Mahadho: Sooyaalkii iyo Waxqabadkii Maxamed Xaashi Dhamac 'Gaarriye'.* Hargeysa: Hal-Aqoon Publishers.

Fabb, N. (2015). *What is Poetry: Language and Memory in the Poems of the World.* Cambridge: Cambridge University Press.

Johnson, J. (1979). Somali prosodic systems. *Horn of Africa 2*(3), 46–54.

Johnson, J. (1996). Musico-moro-syllabic relationships in the scansion of somali oral poetry. In R. Hayward and I. Lewis (Eds.), *Voice and Power: The Culture of Language in North-East Africa. Essays in Honour of B.W. Andrzejewski*, Number 3 in African Languages and Cultures Supplement, pp. 73–82. London: School of Oriental and African Studies.

Kirk, J. (1905). *A Grammar of the Somali Language with Examples in Prose and Verse and an Account of the Yibir and Midgan Dialects.* Cambridge: Cambridge University Press.

Maxamed Xaashi Dhamac 'Gaarriye' (1976a). Miisaanka maansada. *Xiddigta Oktoobar 7th February,* 3.

Maxamed Xaashi Dhamac 'Gaarriye' (1976b). Miisaanka maansada. *Xiddigta Oktoobar 17th January,* 3.

Orwin, M. (2001). On consonants in somali metrics. *Afrikanistische Arbeitspapiere 65*(1), 103–27.

Orwin, M. (2005). On the concept of 'definitive text' in somali poetry. *Oral Tradition 20*(2), 278–299.

Orwin, M. and Maxamed Cabdullaahi Riiraash (1997). An approach to relationships between somali metre types. *African Languages and Cultures 10*(1), 83–100.

Orwin, M. and Mohamed Hashi Dhama 'Gaarriye' (2010). *Peace and Milk, Drought and War,* Chapter Virtual Geminates in the Metre of Somali Poetry, pp. 245–258. London: Hurst and Company.

Rashiid Sheekh Cabdillaahi Xaaji Axmed, translated by Martin Orwin with help from Maxamed Xasan 'Alto', c. b. A. and Ismaaciil Aw Aadan (Eds.) (2009). *War and Peace: an Anthology of Somali Literature. Suugaanta Nabadda iyo Colaadda.* London and Pisa: Progressio and Ponte Invisibile.

How I Met Somali Literature

Khainga O'Okwemba

Kenya Broadcasting Corporation
khaingao@yahoo.com

Abstract

In 2012 I made a return trip to Djibouti to reunite with old friends. I was one of a handful of journalists invited to the conference on the 40th anniversary of the institutionalization of the Somali-language script. I had visited this beautiful, sun-drenched Muslim country four years earlier. Then, I was struck by the friendliness and amiable demeanour of her people. I remember the influential Somali novelist and cultural scholar Dr Maxamed Daahir Afrax and Djiboutian poet Aaden Xasan Aaden taking me to a music concert one night at the People's Palace, as the national theatre is known. After some time, Aaden pulled me aside and said: 'You can walk from your hotel at any time of night. So come and enjoy music from the Horn of Africa. Nothing will happen to you!' I had lived in Nairobi from the days I was a young boy to know that there were places that were considered 'dangerous', even during the day, places where you could be mugged and stripped naked, places where hoodlums could stab you with a knife and leave you for dead if you did not have money or a gold watch or a chain or something valuable to part with!

Back when I was growing up and both dictation and cities fascinated me (for we were sometimes required to memorize) Johannesburg was the one city in Africa that blended admiration and frightful images in my mind. We knew Johannesburg as the most dangerous city on the continent. Although it was renowned as big and developed, crime, rape and murder were all terms we used for its description. It also conjured up images of the colour bar, and, when I read South African writer Alex la Guma's celebratory, bleak novel *A Walk in the Night*, I knew that marauding youths responded in their fashion to cope with the torments of everyday travails of poverty, a forbidding condition which was compounded by the stark brutality of apartheid in Nelson Mandela's homeland, he, the black pimpernel, whose footmark overshadowed the system. Alex la Guma's depiction of squalor in Cape Town's District Six: grim, wanton death, the callousness, the depravity, the inhumanity of the system and the denial of life, as represented by the murderous Constable Raalt, was telling: an African city, nay, a walk in the night, was something to be avoided at all costs, otherwise, it could only mean defiance! It was this defiance that Mandela defended. In the 1980s in Nairobi's Eastlands you came to grips with the term *geng'i* for gang! Why was Djibouti the exception?

The blithe display of stacks of thousands of Djiboutian francs and hundreds of America's green bills on the streets by women providing foreign exchange services late into the night to visitors was, for me, a moment of renunciation. Nobody dared snatch from these women the 'vaults', purses, that at any one time would be holding thousands of Djiboutian francs and US dollars. Crime was almost non-existent in this Muslim society. A young Djiboutian law student filled me in: his preference was to work with international organizations such as the UN after graduating. 'Why not practice at home?' I asked. The chances of succeeding as a criminal lawyer were nil, where would he get clients? 'Why was this so?' I pressed on. Well, it was because a good Muslim was careful not to go against the teachings of Islam rather than be afraid of the punishment meted out in secular law. Crime rates were low! This is the country I was going to visit again.

At the Jomo Kenyatta International Airport, Nairobi, on my way, there was a little matter which distracted my attention from the salience of the metaphysical world, I mean, from the book I was reading. There was a young Kenyan lady who was traveling in the company of three horrid, young men who, I learned, were from a West African country. From their talk and action, I noticed one cast himself as the lady's lover. However, the guy did not reveal himself as a caring man, rather he was mean and degrading. The man's treatment of the Kenyan lady was without tenderness. When the men confabbed, it was in their vernacular, leaving the lady hungry for knowing! 'I sympathize with that lady, see how the man is bossing her around!' I cried to the person next to me. 'It's none of our business,' the pitiless woman retorted. It was none of our business indeed! I feared for that lady as the two of us left home.

My first article from Djibouti was from observation and an interview I had had with Ms Degmo Maxamed Isaaq, then the Secretary General of the National Union of Women. Affable, free-spirited and activist-oriented, Degmo spoke passionately about progress in curbing female circumcision, women in power, academia and public service, and she reminded me that the Head of the Supreme Court of Justice was a woman: Justice Khadija Ababa. To womenfolk she said, 'Women's representation in institutions of governance and policy agencies did not come on a silver platter: it was as a result of spirited campaigns and lobbying.' A few blocks from this woman's office was a girls' school where I would be taken to give a talk on writing! Who said Muslims do not educate girls?

However, it was during that visit in 2009 to Djibouti, at the invitation of Dr Maxamed Daahir Afrax, the founding President of Somali-Speaking PEN that I encountered Somali literature. I began to immerse myself in the cultural history of the Somalis to try to understand the anguish of a people who were fragmented into different geographical enclaves rendering many Somalis minorities in the new countries such as Kenya and Ethiopia. The Somalis, an essentially homogenous society, were fragmented into five different parts: Djibouti, Ethiopia, Kenya, Somalia Italiana, and British Somaliland. Yet hued in the menacing brutality of Constable Raalt, and the plunder of African resources, there was another grimmer legacy of colonialism: divide and rule. The celebrated Somali novelist Nuruddin Farah has reacted to this history: 'I began writing—in the hope of enabling the Somali child at least to characterise his [or her] otherness—and to point at himself [or herself] as the unnamed, the divided other, a schizophrenic child living in the age of colonial contradiction.' (Nuruddin Farah, 1993: p.32).

During this visit Dr Afrax invited me to join the editorial board of *Halabuur: Journal of Somali Literature and Culture*. The soft-spoken Somali intellectual and cultural activist then gifted me with copies of the journal and books. I collected several books on Somali literature, culture and history. I read critical studies on the socio-political novels of Dr Afrax in Kapteijns (1994): *Maanafay* (the name of main character), *Galti-Macruuf* (Camel-Driver Politics) and *Guur-ku-sheeg* (Pseudo-marriage) and the historical essays of Nuruddin Farah such as 'Childhood of my Schizophrenia' (Nuruddin Farah, 1993). *Hal-Abuur* introduced me to Somali literature. I encountered authorities on Somali cultural history such as B.W. Andrzejewski and Lidwien Kapteijns. I read poetry, drama, short stories, essays, reviews and critical studies. I met writers too!

Kapteijns and Ali (1999) for example examine oral literature among Somali women and proceed to advance a theoretical framework for the study of women's literature. They pose the question: is women's literature a tool for 'resistance' as advocated by de Hernandez et al. (2010). Should this literature be seen as 'diagnostic of power' relations between men and women? Perhaps women's literature is well appreciated as a 'subordinate discourse' a form of expression that coexists with a dominant ideology even though they differ in their form and production. However, the 'subordinate' does not imply a 'lesser' form of articulation. It exists as a distinctive form of expression which does not draw attention to itself as an ideology of resistance, hence it remains sufficiently unnoticed by the dominant order to avoid suppression. When I read Nuruddin's essay, 'Of tamarind and cosmopolitanism' (Nuruddin Farah, 2007), I began to understand the historical presence inherent in a modern-day Somali businessman in Nairobi's Eastleigh and his spread of capital in contemporary Kenya.

Hitherto I could entertain the partial narrative of the pirate and buccaneer as the main source of Somali capital. Nuruddin Farah in an interview (The Books Cafe, transmitted at 14:00 on 27 February 2016) rubbishes the pirate story as a hoax invented by some rapacious businessmen in the West to fleece the insurer. But it is his historicization of the civil war in his motherland which he sees as the routing of 'cosmopolitanism' and not the mere collapse of government and the disintegration of Mogadishu that I find enchanting. Cosmopolitanism is a confluence: people of differing backgrounds coexisting and living in harmony. That is what Somalis have lost. The tribal bigots in politics in Africa have not come to grips with the concept of cosmopolitanism as articulated by the Somali writer. The politics of exclusion based on tribal affiliation is Africa's greatest undoing. Because corruption is unabated by those in power, a majority of the populace is left behind if not out on the fringes, thus creating the undercurrents that fuel protest and civil strife.

I heard also for the first time the legends of two historical women in Somali orature: Muuniso and Arraweelo. It is said that one day, Muuniso, the first and only known woman in Northern Somalia to have risen to the position of imam, was hurrying to the mosque to conduct prayers when she met a radiant and energetic young man: '[his] hands strayed / Into her pink bra / And her tremulous hands / Found [his] red shorts / It was time / [They] danced' (O'Okwemba, 2011: pp.89-90). Muuniso did not make it in time for the prayers and so she was relieved of her lofty position. This is what Kapteijns and Ali (1999: p.46) have said: 'Muuniso was on the way to the mosque to lead prayers. However, when she saw the devil's virile member emerge from below the dirt on the path, she could not resist it.' The male priest is as inspired by the sight of a beautiful woman as she is by his sight. This is true today when the Catholic Church is grappling with the issue of celibacy in its parishes. The fact that our female imam was highly educated is relative. Her mistake was absolute. But this is a form of gender discrimination where pleasurable norms are used to cast women as weak and incapable of holding public office. It is important to note that for Muuniso to have been elected an imam at a time when the African and the Muslim society was supposedly a patriarchy speaks volumes about the abilities, aspirations, struggles and achievements of women in the evolution of society.

The story of the legendary Queen Arraweelo, who engineers a domestic strike, catches the men folk napping and assumes the reins of power, is not only a cautionary tale (Kapteijns and Ali, 1999) but is inspiring, especially, when told from a woman's point of view, as opposed to the male's perspective, which confines it to the evil design of a disobedient woman who usurps a man's position in society. Somali women make pilgrimages to the grave of Queen Arraweelo along the coast of the Gulf of Aden to 'place green branches and fresh flowers ... as a sign of respect.' (Ahmed Artan Hanghe quoted in Kapteijns and Ali, 1999: p.40). On the other hand, men 'throw a stone on to the grave and utter a curse.' (Ahmed Artan Hanghe quoted in Kapteijns and Ali, 1999: p.40). What were the conditions that prompted Queen Arraweelo to act the way she did? I know from my interactions with Farah M. Mohamed, author of Queen Arraweelo, that her ascendance to leadership was natural, as she was the one that appealed to her people.

When I returned to Djibouti in 2012, I had read a great deal of Somali literature. Somali country was familiar, one that brought a feeling of déjà vu in me! Yet this trip was unique and special. Save for the galaxy of variegated local and international scholars I was going to meet, there was something in the form of a memorabilia that awaited me. When I left Nairobi, nobody had warned me of the recognition and honour that awaited me for my little contribution in writing about Somali literature and culture in my column, Literary Postcard in *The Star* newspaper. I was given a trophy, which I carried home! It was at the conference that I met the director of the famous Hargeysa International Book Fair, Dr Jama Musse Jama and renowned Italian linguist Prof. Giorgio Banti among others. The conference was marked with celebration and careful appraisal of the institutionalization of the Somali language script since 1972. Once again, writers and intellectuals under the auspices of Somali-Speaking PEN were at the centre of things.

Founded in London by Dr Afrax, Said Saleh and Amina Muuse Weheliye, Somali-Speaking PEN shares in its origins with PEN International's Writers for Peace Committee which was founded in the 1980s as a response to the Cold War that had made it difficult for writers and intellectuals across the East-West divide to collaborate. The founders recognized the need to bring intellectuals together to share and exchange ideas. 'We had the same ideals when we founded Somali Speaking PEN. However, I feared that it would soon collapse because the obstacles were numerous. Today, when I look back, and see the enthusiasm and the energy of the young generation, I feel happy,' Dr Afrax would tell me on the sidelines of the conference as we sat on the patio of a cafeteria having tea. This conference was huge, not only because all the presidents of the splinter nations of the Somali territories were present, but because all the major Somali intellectuals and scholars participated.

The conference was held at the University of Djibouti. 'Whenever the legendary Maxamed Ibraahin Warsame 'Hadraawi', described as the greatest living Somali poet, walked from the conference hall, he was mobbed by the crowd.' Thats how I annotated my essay when I first met Hadraawi in Djibouti in 2012. I would sue for an interview. But it was difficult to get Hadraawi that day, as the frenzied mob threw a cauldron around him, taking 'selfies' with the legend, at a time when the phenomenon was not so much in vogue. A student at the university, who knew me as one of a handful of literary journalists covering the conference, scrapped me through to Hadraawi. The legend stopped to hear my plea but it was drowned in the cacophony! However, Hadraawi took my notebook, and in there, using his pen, left a squiggle, a symbol, an image, or was it an autograph? And that was Hadraawi, instructive!

But where was the poetry of this great African? Because he wrote in Somali, I would wait for another three years when Dr Jama invited me to his homeland in Somaliland at the First Somali Linguistics Workshop held at the Hargeysa Cultural Centre. The broad thematic concern was edited to include 'Literature', so I was asked to give a brief talk on how I met Somali literature. On the eve before I left Somaliland, I went to Dr Jama and asked if I could interview him for The Books Café literature programme which I present on the Kenya Broadcasting Corporation. He said, 'You must be tired now; I didnt see you go for lunch. Let's do the interview later in the evening.' Dr Jama had watched me skip lunch to conduct interviews with participants at the workshop. True to his words Dr Jama came to pick me up at the hotel alongside Swedish linguist Dr Morgan Nilsson and we drove to his home, which is also 'a writer's asylum house' or a writer's guest house if you wish, where English linguist Dr Martin Orwin of SOAS University of London was busy working. It was here that Dr Jama went into his library and pulled out a copy of a book I will live to cherish: *Hadraawi: The Poet and The Man* (Jama Musse Jama, 2013). This is the book that I read on my way home from Hargeysa.

Therein is the poem, 'Has Love Been Blood-Written?' (translated by Martin Orwin).

love was a food store
which when it was heated
with charcoal and fire
the glowing embers
of emotions stirred
did they fill a large pot
time after time
drag the enclosure's
night-time gate
each one with tender eyes
seeing nothing harmed the other
did they listen thus

... if self sacrifice is not made
the breath of life not exchanged
if one does not wait
for an enduring legacy
the building of a house upright
children and earthly sustenance
then the kisses and intentions
are nothing but superficial
... a poison sipped to satisfaction
in that one same moment
like hyenas snatching
a girl of good repute
as they hide themselves
in the *higlo* tree.

This is the Somali that I know; a site of knowledge production. This poem is philosophical. What is love? Were the two in love? Or was it infatuation? Hadraawi's greatness as a poet lies with his vision of reality, his masterful use of language, his stunning imagery and metaphor, his remarkable deployment of juxtaposition, his affirmation that 'poetry has an element of absolute beauty,' (Khainga 2011). There's something else: his association with the vulnerable, the downtrodden, the afflicted. Like most of Hadraawi's love poems, this poem transcends the intimate relationship between man and woman. The poet is telling us to be wary of deception.

Hadraawi would be a thorn in the flesh of rogue politicians. In his poem 'Clarity' (translated by Said Jama and W.N. Herbert.), he writes, 'My horse is Clarity / I won't hobble it / But here I set it at ease.' A conscientious man, truthful to the lofty ideals of justice, freedom and goodness, Hadraawi warned his countrymen of 'a strange disease of vision' in reference to the political elite's blinding tribalism, looting and corruption, which would 'despoil the nation.' Hadraawi juxtaposes government's 'tapping drum' with a writer's 'clarion bell.' Did Hadraawi foretell the disintegration of the Somali state? 'Then I am that prediction / of clouds still to come / bringing a downpour / that will cover the whole country.'

Indeed, Hadraawi's lines, as in his own words are 'as striking as the stripes of an oryx / as visible and as lovely.' But it was 'The Killing of the She-Camel' in 1972, in which Hadraawi calls the plunderers 'aardvark', that the discredited political regime was alerted to a dissident voice. Hadraawi was arrested in 1973 and imprisoned without trial. Many Somalis were alarmed by the poet's incarceration. Prominent personalities took up the matter of his release with General Siad Barre. The General consented only on the condition that Hadraawi would make a written request for pardon and pledge to refrain from any further criticism of government. A demand which Hadraawi dismissed outright as outrageous: '... when laughter becomes a crime / our country has unfinished business.' (Translated by Said Jama, Mohamed Hasan 'Alto' and W.N. Herbert.) Thus the people's poet was jailed for five years until 1978. Hadraawi articulated the 'mother tongue' issue long before the disingenuous jumped on the band wagon. The Nobel Prize does not give us the best there is, for as English scholar, Dr Martin Orwin, observes, 'Hadraawi is one of the world's major living poets.' Thus Dr Afrax (Halabuur 1993) has observed that 'Somali literature chronicles ... all significant historical events. It's the factual mirror in which the Somali finds an intimate representation of himself.'

Literature transcends barriers. This is the reason I appealed to visiting linguists: Prof. Banti, Dr Orwin, Dr Nilsson and Somaliland linguist Prof. Mohamed H. Raabi that they should find it worthwhile to help the remarkable Hargeysa Cultural Centre in translating more Somali literature into different languages so that this literature can be read and appreciated by the rest of humanity.

What's more, Somalis have a saying that when someone helps you, she does not expect you to thank them, yet it would be un-Kenyan not to imprint in my diary the names of the visionary Somali intellectuals, the resourceful Dr Afrax, Dr Jama, Aden, true sons of Africa. Gentlemen, I doff my hat!

Bibliography

de Hernandez, J. B., P. Dongala, O. Jolaosho, and A. Serafin (Eds.) (2010). *African Women Writing Resistance: Contemporary Voices.* Madison: The University of Wisconsin Press.

Jama Musse Jama (Ed.) (2013). *Maxamed Ibraahin Warsame 'Hadraawi': The Poet and the Man (Volume 1).* Pisa: Ponte Invisibile (redsea-online) and The Poetry Translation Centre.

Kapteijns, L. (1994). A window on somali society: The novels of maxamed d afrax. *Hal-Abuur 1*(2 & 3), 50–58.

Kapteijns, L. and M. O. Ali (1999). *Women's Voices in a Man's World: Women and the Pastoral Tradition in Northern Somali Orature, c. 1899–1980.* Portsmouth, NH: Heinemann.

Nuruddin Farah (1993). Childhood of my schizophrenia. *Hal-Abuur 1*(2 & 3), 30–32.

Nuruddin Farah (2007). Of tamarind and cosmopolitanism. *Hal-Abuur 2*(1 & 2), 34–37.

O'Okwemba, K. (2011). *Smiles in Pathos and Other Poems.* Nsemia Inc. Publishers.

Printed in the United States
By Bookmasters